EXPERIENCING DISPLAYS

by RITA KOHN

THE SCARECROW PRESS, INC.
Metuchen, N.J., & London ❧ 1982

Also by Rita Kohn:

JESSE FELL: PLANTER OF CITIES
    Normal, Illinois: The Normalite, 1968

YOU CAN DO IT: A PR Skills Manual for Librarians, with Krysta A. Tepper
    Metuchen, New Jersey: Scarecrow Press, 1981

HAVE YOU GOT WHAT THEY WANT? A Workbook of Public Relations
    Strategies for the School Librarian/Media Specialist, with Krysta A.
    Tepper
    Metuchen, New Jersey: Scarecrow Press, 1982

Library of Congress Cataloging in Publication Data

Kohn, Rita T.
   Experiencing displays.

   Includes index.
   1. Library exhibits--Handbooks, manuals, etc.
I. Title.
Z717.K63   020'.74   82-3187
ISBN 0-8108-1534-6   AACR2

To
Walter

in honor of twenty-five years
and our three best experiences:
Sharon, Martin, and Thomas,

and

To the Normal Public Library,
on whose Board Walter Kohn served for twelve years

TABLE OF CONTENTS

ACKNOWLEDGMENTS

This book appears without a bibliography because no written works were consulted during its composition. This is not to say, however, that the literature on displays, whether geared toward merchandising, industrial shows, or libraries did not have an influence on the formation of ideas or on an approach that appears in the following pages. Thus, to anyone who has written on the subject of displays, I acknowledge a debt of gratitude.

In the same way, libraries across the United States, Canada, and Western Europe have had some impact because in visiting them I have carried away impressions that naturally will have surfaced in my approach to the subject of displays. Likewise, retail establishments, through their displays, have added to my development of a philosophy.

Specific references to books and places are made in the text. Nevertheless, I will underscore my appreciation to the staffs of the Normal Public Library, the San Francisco Public Library, and the University High School Media Center/Library for permitting me to take photographs.

Harold Pines of Bloomington/Normal deserves a word of acknowledgment because I learned something very valuable about retailing displays through an association with his stores. The brief but poignant philosophical discussions with Nathan Deitch, owner of Sabrina's of Normal and Bloomington, have had a bearing on my thinking regarding the direction in which library displays can go.

To Ruth Cobb and Sharon Kohn I offer up a hearty thank you for their comments on the manuscript.

To friends, including the Gordons, Hirts, Reisingers, Schrenzels, and Woodsons, and to colleagues in the College of Continuing Education and Public Service at Illinois State University I say "Thank You for your support and understanding."

But the bulk of appreciation goes to my family. To Walter, for his steadfast faith that the work was worthwhile and that a clean house isn't an essential ingredient to a year's worth of living; to Sharon, who never complained about my not writing letters to keep her in touch with family happenings; to Martin, for his unfailing good humor during my times of dismal doubt; to Tom, because he kept the household together and the dust from taking over even when other demands on him were great; to Shirley and Paul, who opened up their home and their hearts so that I could have the peace of mind to tackle both a new career and a new book within the same time frame.

Rita Kohn

Normal, Illinois

September 27, 1981

LIST OF ILLUSTRATIONS

INTRODUCTION

"We need help with displays," said librarian after librarian during the initial round of visits following my appointment as Public Relations Consultant to the Corn Belt Library System, then located in Bloomington, Illinois.

"What kind of help?" I asked.

"Ideas."

Librarians recognize the functions of displays as catalysts for increased circulation, as enticements for browsing, and as purveyors of the library messages. Librarians also know that in order to do a good job with displays they need time and money-- both in perpetual short supply.

The challenge has been to come up with a plan of action that substitutes creativity for the best that money can buy. I refuse to succumb to patterns because, while it's easy to trace and cut, doing it on a steady basis robs the soul of its rights of growth.

Borrowing from the precepts of both theatre and retail merchandising, I've coined an acronym that synthesizes the basic FACTS of displays:

Focus, for the audience and on the product
Active, so as to involve the viewer
Creative, so as to present the familiar in a
     new way
Timely, to be of interest because of the season
     an event, or a special interest
Sophistication, to elevate the audience and the
     product

To move from philosophy to action, I suggest that librarians think in terms of shapes to provide themselves with limitless ideas and a fairly easy way to carry out those ideas.

The world--nature and man-made objects--is composed of items that are made up of the basic shapes--circles, squares, rectangles, and triangles. If you need proof, stroll through a playground. Seesaws are rectangular planks balanced on a system of metal cylinders. Swings are rectangular boards attached by round link chains to a triangular base. Merry-go-rounds are just that--rounds or circles.

While you're out, squint up at the sun. It comes out circular with rectangular beams.

Examine flowers. Isn't it amazing that their components are modifications of the basic shapes?

A truck drives by and suddenly you see it as a combination of squares and circles. Children run past, and they, too, neatly fit into squares for bodies, circles for heads, rectangles for limbs.

Browse in stores, being receptive to shapes. Suddenly you're bombarded. Out comes your pad and soft lead pencil. The ideas spill out. Baskets, frames, boxes, pockets, hats, table settings, pots and pans all suggest possibilities.

You know what needs to be put on display. You merely need ideas as to how to put together a display that will accomplish your goals. Physically, displays can be two-dimensional or three-dimensional. Which option you use at a given time and place will depend on the theme and materials in addition to the audience and space.

The approach of this guide is to share with you the stimulus that I receive from shapes. The challenge is for you to grow as a result of this sharing. There is one message that I am underlining. It is to provide a sense of unity throughout the library. Rather than confuse the patron with a mixed bag, develop one theme to carry out throughout the departments.

Planning is important. Take the time to think through your goals. Identify the library materials, programs, and services you want "to put on display" in your library. Determine what space can be utilized for displays.

This book does not appear in chapters. It is journey through stimuli. Like displays, it is an unfolding, an expanding, a revealing, a disclosing, a spreading before view. Scan the whole book before you begin to read in earnest. You will discover that display objects are saved and used in different ways. You will discover, too, that as you gain confidence in your ability to create in an art form that must communicate a clear-cut message (with or without words), you'll see combinations of display techniques and make thematic connections that are unique to you.

Each section:

1) states a general objective, which is the reason for mounting the display throughout the library;

2) offers ideas as adjuncts to the display, which become activities that are spin-offs from the theme; and

3) provides a discussion on how, what, where, why, when, and who of the display itself, which is a technique and materials aid.

An evaluation procedure is not repeated with each section. It is generally understood that each activity has specific objectives that come under the general objective. The evaluation is a process of examining how well the specific objectives have been met. This procedure can be formal, as with patrons filling out questionnaires, or informal, as with random conversations with patrons.

The goal of this book has been to remain open-ended, so that you, the reader, truly grow through the experience. Ingenuity is simply taking something old and presenting it in a unique manner.

DISPLAY IDEAS
AND THEIR
IMPLEMENTATION

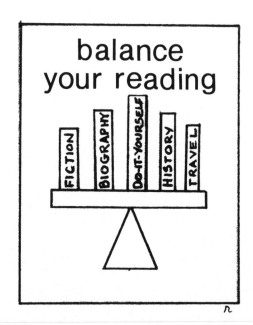

Illus. 1.   SEESAW MONTAGE

SEESAW

Objective of the display:

To help patrons be aware of the wide variety of library materials.

Adjuncts to the display:

A new introduction to the library--its materials, services, and programs--
in bookmark form and on cassette tape for visually handicapped patrons.

An article in the local newspaper describing the variety of library materials.

Posters placed in strategic locations in the community.   (See Illus. 2.)

Discussion of the display:

Balance came to mind when I observed people on the seesaw.

DIFFERENT INTERESTS BALANCE US   TILT THE SCALES IN YOUR FAVOR

BALANCE YOUR READING   USE YOUR LIBRARY

BALANCE YOUR LIFE THROUGH
READING

A stylized three-dimensional display of everything in the library can reproduce the seesaw scene.   Make an "H" out of three pieces of wood. Glue a piece of sturdy styrofoam to one of the longer sides.   After it dries, cover the whole structure with felt (flannel is fine, too).   (See Illus. 3.)

In Illus. 4, the being on the left is a block of styrofoam covered with a book jacket.   Anchored into the styrofoam is a disc.   The arms are rolled-up magazines, the legs, rolled-up newspapers, each anchored to the styrofoam body with large decorator pins.   The styrofoam book is pinned to the styrofoam layer on the board.

The being on the right is a tape talking-book case. The take-up reel head fits over the sides of the case and is snug. The arm is a rolled-up government document, the leg a rolled-up poster. They are pinned to the case. (If this mutilates a case, use styrofoam that is covered to look like a talking-book case.)

The display shown in Illus. 5 works for tabletop, shelf-top, or in a glass case, where you can set it up on a shelf and eliminate the "H" form (set a covered brick under the shelf to make it seem as though the shelf is balanced over the brick). Place the caption on the shelf above.

If you want to carry the balance idea into the browsing area or the YA-bookshelf area, create a stylized balance (rectangle over triangle) and line rectangles, with categories affixed to them, atop the horizontal rectangle. (See Illus. 6.) Use flannel or felt shapes that are affixed to a three-part hinged screen that is covered with flannel. (See Illus. 7.) This is a handy informational device. You'll enjoy using it in a dozen different ways.

For a two-dimensional effect on a bulletin board, pin a styrofoam triangle and a styrofoam rectangle to the backing. Roll book jackets so that the two sides are tucked under the spine. (See Illus. 8.) Pin these to the backing. The styrofoam shapes should be covered. Either burlap or flannel is a good, all-purpose choice. (See Illus. 9.)

You can expand the idea to "sell" large-print books by putting the large-print edition on one end and the regular-print edition on the other end of a seesaw facsimile and add the tag line:

LARGE-PRINT BOOKS WEIGH THE SAME AS REGULAR-PRINT BOOKS

Assemble a variety of building toys, including Tinker Toys, Lincoln Logs, or Fischer-Price building blocks. Put them into seesaw structures. Intersperse library materials. Or bring in balance toys. Set them up to be in motion. Elevate them (covered cans are great for this kind of display) and place library materials around. Add a sign:

UP OR DOWN, THE LIBRARY IS THERE

Take the idea in another direction. Approach balance scientifically. Invite a display of balancing instruments, compliments of your high school science department.

Invite the local photography shop or photography club to sponsor a display of photographs that catch people in the act of balancing or that record objects that are balanced.

Invite a mini-science fair on "balance." Display the items people put together.

Artisans may enjoy the challenge of creating banners on the theme "Balance Your Life Through Reading" or "Different Interests Balance Us."

Place the banners about the library. Arrange for a purchase prize of the best one, two, or three entries.

All of the above ideas are grist for the publicity mill. You can get a lot of media coverage and thus tell the story, too, of the wide variety of library materials that are available for the asking.

Now, what comes to your mind?

Illus. 2. POSTER: "TILT THE SCALES IN YOUR FAVOR"

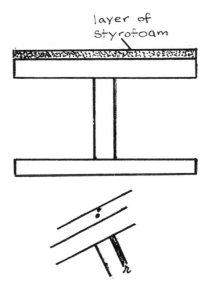

Illus. 3.   "H" FORM (DETAIL)

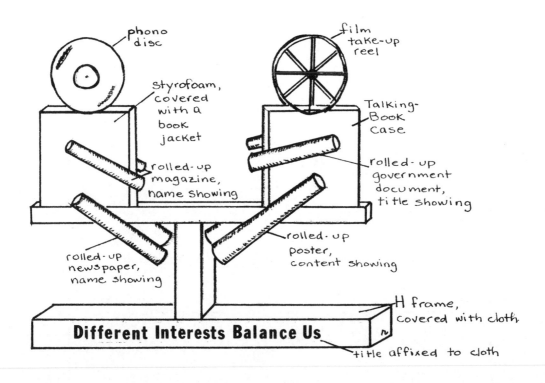

Illus. 4.   3-D DISPLAY: "DIFFERENT INTERESTS BALANCE US"

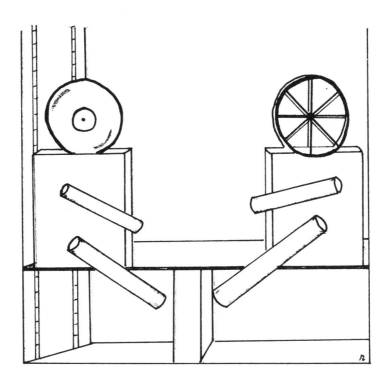

Illus. 5.   CASE DISPLAY: "DIFFERENT
INTERESTS BALANCE US"

Illus. 6.   2-D DISPLAY: "BALANCE YOUR READING"

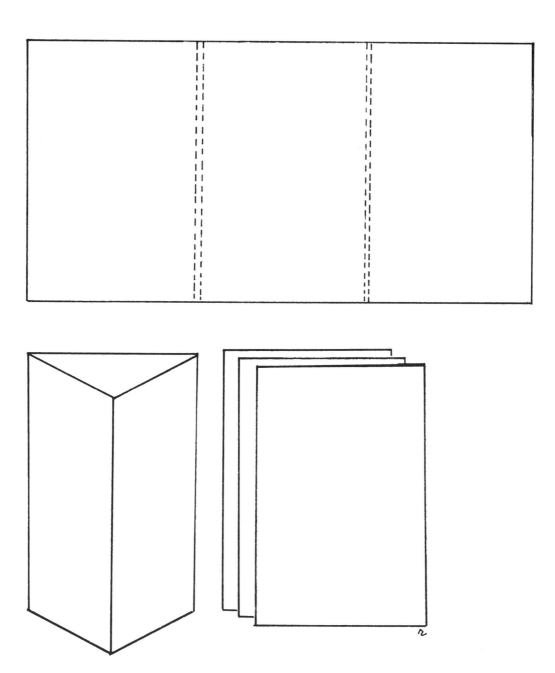

Illus. 7. FLANNEL- OR FELT-COVERED SCREEN OF THREE PANELS

Illus. 9.   2-D DISPLAY: "BALANCE YOUR LIFE
THROUGH READING"

Illus. 8.   ROLLED BOOK
JACKET (DETAIL)

HOURGLASS

Objective of the display:

To show that the library is a good use of time.

Adjuncts to the display:

Bibliographies especially geared toward research needs, voice-over books, spoken books, unusual titles (for a change of pace), books with a "time" theme.

Programs on research techniques; the meaning of time as perceived by scientists (relativity), poets, very young people, elderly people, composers, farmers, industrialists (time studies), runners; evolution of clocks.

Discussion of the display:

The sand timer gets used every day for the three-minute egg. One day the egg gets hard-cooked, the pot sizzles (just short of being scorched). This leads to all sorts of ideas, including:

TIME RUNNING OUT ON YOUR TERM PAPER?
GET HELP AT YOUR LIBRARY

NO TIME FOR READING?
LISTEN TO OUR SOLUTION

TIME FOR A CHANGE OF PACE!

WHAT IS TIME?

TIME MOVES ON

OUR TIME IS YOURS
ASK US

TIME TO SPARE?
JOIN OUR LIBRARY
VOLUNTEERS

Bring in some sand timers, place them on a surface, make a sign with the caption TIME FOR A CHANGE OF PACE!, and put out a variety of books that will be of immediate interest to your clientele.

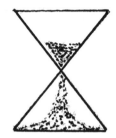

**TIME running out
on your Term Paper?**

**Get Help
at your LIBRARY**

TIME FOR
A CHANGE
OF PACE!

Illus. 10.   TIMER MONTAGE

For a poster that speaks directly to students, especially at midterm, ask a direct question. Place the poster where young people will see it. This is also an easy flyer to make. If you can find out ahead of time what the general assigned topics are, bring those books out on a cart, shelf-top, table, or wherever to be readily available. Provide guides for research techniques and reference tools. (See Illus. 10.)

Use the sand-timer theme to highlight voice-over books, books on disc, dramatized readings on tape or disc, and so on. This may also be an opportune time to describe the good care of tapes and discs. You could also arrange for a display of players, courtesy of local electronics stores. Draw attention to the display with a sign. (See Illus. 11.) Add to it by placing tools, dusting aids, cooking and baking utensils, iron, needlework, etc., around the display so that people get the idea that they can use their time in double duty.

Line up a progression of sand timers (see Illus. 12) as an introduction to your library's history collection--local and general. Illus. 13 is a diagram to assist you in making a "Time Moves On" sign. Pull out photographs, memorabilia, and artifacts. Draw a time line with significant dates.

Underscore your staff's reason for being there by announcing it with a notice (see Illus. 14) on the circulation desk. Invite volunteers through a poster. (See Illus. 15.) Mount photographs of volunteers at work; place application blanks within easy reach.

Let's take a few minutes to discuss how you can create "timers" that are interesting to viewers and easy for you to make. The hourglass shape itself can be drawn as two triangles or cut out from any kind of paper or cloth. The "sand" can indeed be sand. Apply rubber cement to the paper or cloth "timer" in an area where you want sand to appear. Then sprinkle sand to give a dimensional effect and supply a bit of realism. Sand can also be drawn in. (See Illus. 16.)

Illus. 18 and 19 show another effect you can create, while Illus. 17 suggests using yarn or string with pins to keep the shape you want.

Time, as a theme, does well for a large part of the library collection. Ask "WHAT IS TIME?," put up a number of books with poems that address the theme of time, and provide attractively designed cards or pieces of paper that are imprinted with this message:

TELL WHAT TIME MEANS TO YOU.

Weave the responses into a feature story for the local newspaper or your library's publication.

Issue a list of records in sporting events along with books on sports involving "time." Illustrate "time" in music. Mount a display that describes time signature and demonstrates note values (meter is the preferred term here, but time is the popular term) and tempo. Provide a metronome to indicate the exact tempo of a piece of music. Arrange for anyone who desires to do so to "conduct" an ensemble or a vocal group.

Place time in the context of the culinary arts. Arrange for a display and demonstration of cooking utensils and the effect they have on the time it takes to cook the same item--e.g., wok, pressure cooker, crock pot, steamer, saucepan, microwave oven.

Bring in games that employ a timer. Let people guess how much time it takes to accomplish any variety of tasks that you dream up--e.g., "How much time does it really take to hard-cook an egg?"

This is what I thought up one early morning. What does a sand timer turn _you_ on to?

Illus. 11.   NO TIME FOR READING?   LISTEN FOR A SOLUTION

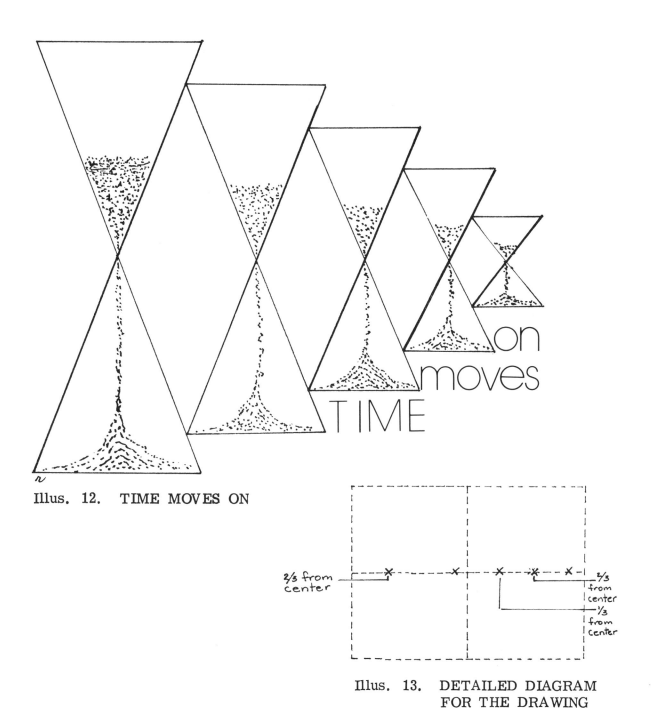

Illus. 12.   TIME MOVES ON

Illus. 13.   DETAILED DIAGRAM
FOR THE DRAWING
OF ILLUSTRATION 12

Illus. 14.   OUR TIME IS YOURS: ASK US

Illus. 15.   TIME TO SPARE?   JOIN OUR LIBRARY
VOLUNTEERS

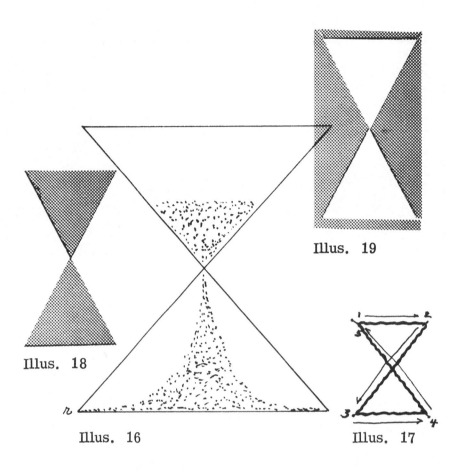

Illus. 19

Illus. 18

Illus. 16

Illus. 17

Illus. 16.   "TIMER" MADE WITH TWO TRIANGLES
AND REAL SAND

Illus. 17.   "TIMER" MADE FROM YARN OR STRING
WITH PINS

Illus. 18.   "TIMER" MADE FROM FABRIC

Illus. 19.   OUTLINE EFFECTS TO SUGGEST TIMER

POCKETS

Objective of the display:

To draw attention to those parts of the collection especially suited to interests and needs of people engaged in a specific activity or of people involved with a general grouping.

Adjuncts to the display:

Bibliographies in categories of general interest to your patrons:

SPORTS (as a general topic and divided into specific sports)
TRAVEL (short day-trips, abroad, historic sites)
REPAIR & OTHER DO-IT-YOURSELF TECHNIQUES (seasonal or general)
SCOUTING-BADGE REQUIREMENTS
YOUNG ADULT MATERIALS (fiction and nonfiction)
BUSINESS & INDUSTRY (the young executive, latest research)
CHILDREN'S

Programs on special interests (you will know what is of particular interest based on your surveys of patrons--"Practical Photography," "Football from the Stands," "Part-time Job Pointers")

Library promo distributed with tickets people buy for events all over the community (sporting events, theater, concerts, films)

```
THIS TICKET GIVES YOU ENTRANCE
TO A LIFETIME OF ENTERTAINMENT
    Present it at _____
    [address]
                    during
    [hours]
YOU'LL GET SOMETHING SPECIAL
```

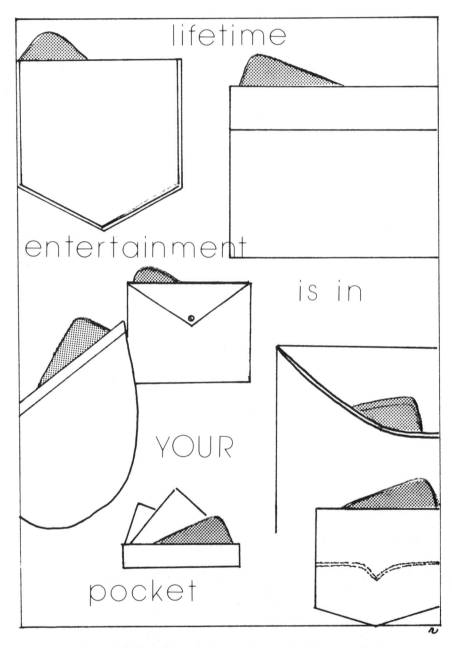

Illus. 20.   LIFETIME ENTERTAINMENT IS IN YOUR POCKET

Place book jackets (and books) and other library materials in retail stores where clothing is on display. Place a library-card mockup in a pocket that is visible.

Arrange for media coverage for the above activities.

Discussion of the display:

Accentuating the pocket brings to mind endless possibilities for displays because pockets tell a great deal about the person. An afternoon of pocket-watching at the library yields pages of sketches. There are several possibilities.

Depending upon the kind of space you have and the kind of rapport possible with local merchants, bringing in garments and placing them in strategic sections of the library is both easy and attention-getting. Illus. 21 is an example of what can be done.

Mannequins, borrowed from a retail shop, work well for storefront libraries or as window displays in libraries with an expanse of glass fronting on pedestrian traffic. The garments on display can be current or period fashions, theater or holiday costumes, or native dress from around the world. The titles poking out of pockets can be people-stoppers because of the association, or the message held by a mannequin can entice passersby into the library.

A clothesline can also serve as a display vehicle by allowing you to pin up clothes with pockets. (Incidentally, you will want to use the clothesline for any number of other display purposes, so keep it within easy reach. A line can be strung up in a window, in the children's section ("Sing a Song of Sixpence, a Pocketful of _____"), or wherever it is appropriate to string up a line. Be certain that safety factors are taken into account. Fit appropriate library items into the pockets.

In addition to, or in place of three-dimensional displays, you can pin items up on walls. Place books that are appropriate to the garment in the pocket(s). You don't even have to put up a caption. Cookbooks in an apron pocket tell it all. (See Illus. 22.) Jeans also fold easily for a wall pinup, and you have two pockets in view to fill with appropriate titles--especially paperbacks. (See Illus. 23.)

Illus. 24 and 25 show the variety of pockets for which library materials can be found. You will find many more "pockets" to fill.

If you want to use the idea of pockets but can't find clothes or the space to display them, make drawings of garments. Illus. 26 demonstrates how you can stylize garments into components of basic shapes. Add dimension by cutting pockets from fabric and stapling them to the drawings. You can place books into these pockets, and of course place other books on the topics of interest nearby so that anyone attracted by the display can find many titles to consider.

The slogan "Pick Our Pockets" permits a variety of display capabilities. Cut pockets, large enough to hold paperback books, from a scrapbox of sturdy fabrics. Staple the pockets securely to a flat surface, such as a bulletin board (see Illus. 27) or a screen (see Illus. 28). Cut the title from fabric, too, using block letters or stencils as the pattern. To encourage "picking of pockets," be certain that the surface is convenient for readers to reach and remove the books. Keep the pockets continuously stocked with paperback titles.

A play on the "pick our pockets" theme involves emphasizing the "circulation pockets" of books. A sign on a table or shelf announcing "Pick Our Pockets" can be surrounded by books, rubber-banded open to show "circulation pockets" with messages placed inside them. The messages can be along these lines: "I'm a Gem. Take Me Home." "Priceless. Examine the Contents." "Invaluable. You'll Be Richly Rewarded." You might also add a display card with an explanation of how and why "book pockets" came about and perhaps provide this as an opportunity for the technical-services librarian to schedule a demonstration of how books are prepared for circulation. Another possibility is a close look at Charles Dickens's Oliver Twist, whose childhood was spent among professional pickpockets. This "occupation" could make for an interesting seminar series.

And, speaking of pockets, who has the most natural one of all? Madame Kangaroo, to be sure! On close observation, one can conclude that kangaroos are a composite of triangles for the upper torso, half-circle for the pouch, and rectangles for the legs and feet. (See Illus. 29.) You can create a display for the children's area by pinning the torso flat to a bulletin board, molding out the pouch to hold book jackets peeking out of the top, and pinning the legs and feet flat. Another possibility is anchoring the torso and legs and feet to a tub or cauldron that holds a variety of books ready for circulation.

Taking off on "classics" and "name brands," draw attention to the fiction section by propping up an oversized "name brand" pocket that is surrounded by books authored by well-known names. (See Illus. 30.)

Pocket possibilities are now in your capable hands. Look over your materials--be they books, magazines, newspapers, discs, tapes, or films-- and place them together with the pockets they best fill. You're merely putting the regular offerings on display in an unusual way, and getting extra attention as a result.

Illus. 21. THE PERFECT ACCESSORY

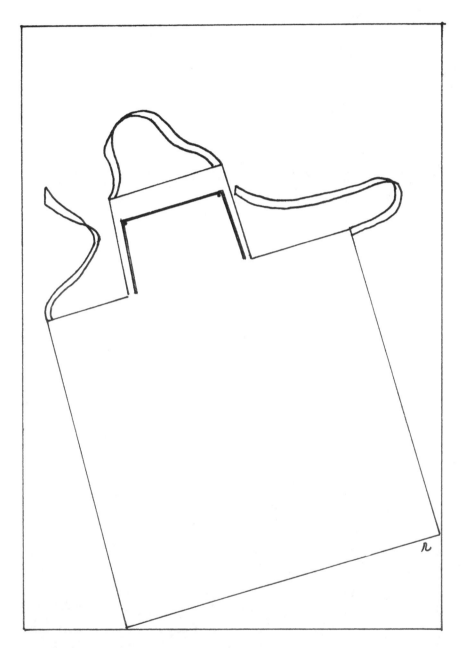

Illus. 22. APRON WITH POCKET

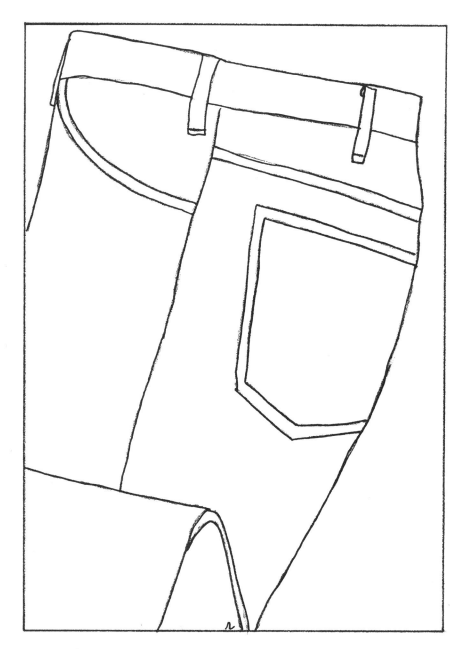

Illus. 23.   JEANS POCKETS

Illus. 24. MEN'S POCKETS

Illus. 25.   CHILDREN'S AND YAs' POCKETS

Illus. 26. STYLIZED DRAWINGS OF GARMENTS WITH POCKETS

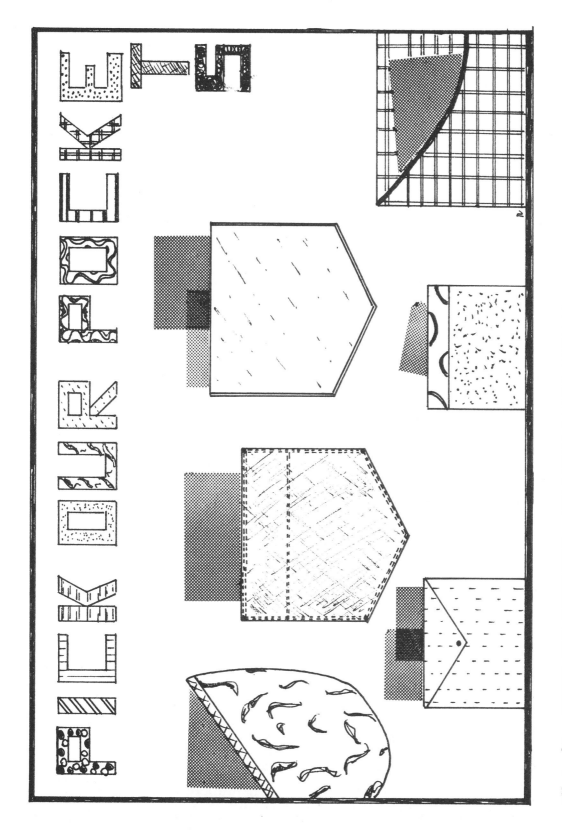

Illus. 27. "PICK OUR POCKETS": BULLETIN BOARD DISPLAY

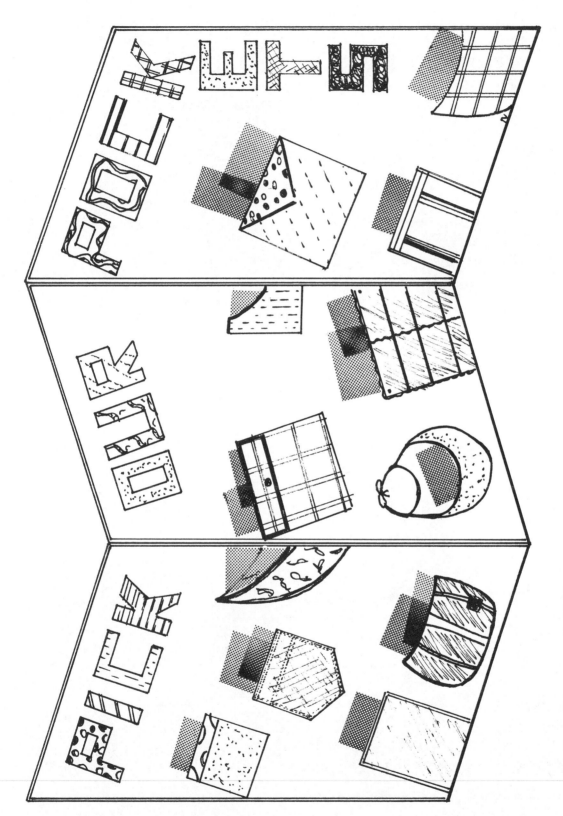

Illus. 28. "PICK OUR POCKETS": SCREEN DISPLAY

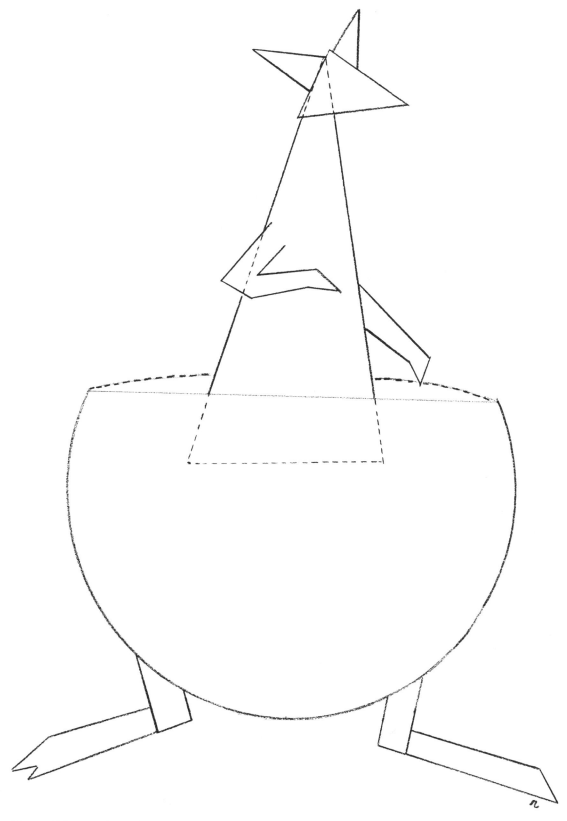

Illus. 29. KANGAROO

put
a
famous name
i̲n̲
your pocket

Illus. 30.   PUT A FAMOUS NAME I̲N̲ YOUR POCKET

FRAMES

Objective of the display:

To highlight "classics," series, and various forms of a theme.

Adjuncts to the display:

This is a great opportunity for sharing. As you will see in the section that follows, I'm suggesting that you ask a frame shop to lend you items from their stock to feature in your library display. You might also offer to provide a display in their shop, on the topic of their choice, using library materials.

Invite a master frame-maker to demonstrate frame-making in the library. Arrange a program on the history of frames. Art historians are a good source.

Set up a program on the arranging and hanging of artwork, family photographs and posters in homes, offices, waiting rooms, etc.

Run a series on books in series from Louisa May Alcott to Agatha Christie to John Galsworthy to L. Frank Baum to anyone on the current popular list. Include a variety of genres. Set it up in any way that is best for your community. You may want to have people read and discuss under the guidance of a leader. You may want to have a series of illustrated lectures with guests who are experts on specific authors.

Provide a noncredit history-of-literature course through the continuing-education department of a nearby university.

Provide a program on the procedure for turning a book into a film, TV production, series, play, or musical.

Arrange for dramatizations or oral readings of "classics" in literature and drama.

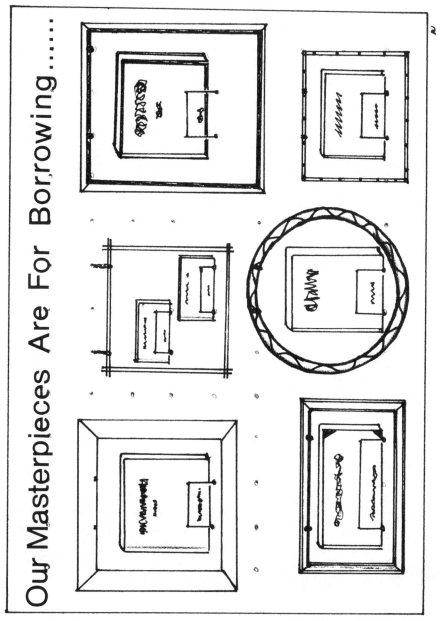

Illus. 31.   OUR MASTERPIECES ARE FOR BORROWING

Arrange a program on nonfiction classics, including cookbooks, books on manners, books on personal growth, or reference books. The guest lecturer can illustrate how these kinds of books made an impact and how changes came about because of them or how certain ideas or customs solidified because of them.

Discussion of the display:

This is an easy display to put up anyplace in the library. Illus. 31 utilizes pegboard wall space. The announcement is straightforward--"Our Masterpieces Are for Borrowing"--and opens the way for you to bring out the truly fine pieces of writing, fiction and nonfiction. You can include prize-winning books, recordings, and films. Brag about all of your materials! Use brackets and hooks to hold the library materials and the frames.

Obviously, you need to borrow frames. With the growth of self-framing shops you will find a source within easy access to your community. You can also invite commercial framers to lend you their wares. Usually, you or your library system or consortium has purchased framed art reproductions from them and they will be willing to cooperate on this venture. Be certain, however, to give credit where it is due and place placards reading: "Frames Courtesy of _____." Any publicity on the display should also note the firms by name.

Illus. 32 shows how hinged standing frames can work for books in series. You can place this part of the display on a table or the top shelf of a low bookcase. If you show such series as the March family, the Forsytes, or the Wilders, you can letter a sign that identifies these books as "Family Portraits."

If you show the works of a particular author, such as Hemingway or Michener or Dickens, or of a playwright, poet, historian, philosopher, writer of science fiction or fantasy, or local writer, the title can read: "Original Works."

Illus. 33 places the hinged frame in an unusual posture so that it becomes a mirror image that shows the book and the recording of it, or it could be an effective way to show the regular-print book and the large-print or talking book.

With Illus. 34, you can move into a new dimension. Here, I suggest that you show the progression of a theme. I've chosen two rather well-known musicals to trace back to their "roots."

Pyramus and Thisbe, a boy and girl living during the reign of Queen Semiramis in ancient Babylon, are star-crossed lovers. William Shakespeare took this spare story and, sometime around 1594 or 1595, wove it into the tragedy Romeo and Juliet. Central to the plot is the enmity of two families.

In A Midsummer Night's Dream, written at about the same time as was Romeo and Juliet, Shakespeare places the story of Pyramus and Thisbe as a play within a play, depicting the events starkly, as they appear in translation from the Greek. The tragedy turns into comedy at the hands of Bottom, the weaver, and company.

Hector Berlioz, in 1839, added a third dimension to the adaptation of the theme with the dramatic symphony, Romeo and Juliet. Charles François Gounod went a step further in writing the opera Roméo et Juliette, which opened in 1867. Two years later, Pëtr Ilich Tchaikovsky set Shakespeare's tragedy to music in the form of an orchestral fantasy-overture. In his own 1935-36 work, Serge Prokofiev sets the story of Romeo and Juliet as a ballet. In 1957, a musical tale exploded on Broadway. The Arthur Laurents/Leonard Bernstein/Stephen Sondheim update, West Side Story, testifies to the durability of the ancient tale and to the progression of genius.

Each of the seven "adaptations" retains the central thread of the lovers, separated in life, united in death. However, each artist has contributed a unique form. To bring this connection to the attention of patrons is a logical aspect of librarianship.

Pygmalion, artist-king of Cyprus, fashioned a statue of a female and ascribed to it all of the virtues he expected in a woman. At the festival in honor of Venus, goddess of love, he dared to ask that one such as Galatea (the name he had given to his creation), be given to him as wife. Venus, understanding his true desire, uses her art to bring the statue to life.

While many allusions to the "woman on the pedestal" image have been made, perhaps most notably by the German poet, dramatist, historian, and philosopher Schiller, in his poem the "Ideals," the best-known borrowing of the Greek fable is George Bernard Shaw's romance in five acts, Pygmalion. Forty-four years later, the gutter-girl Eliza Doolittle becomes the modern-day Galatea in the sparkling musical comedy My Fair Lady. Alan Jay Lerner and Frederick Loewe proved that there is more than one way to portray the Pygmalion prototype.

You might add a dimension on your own by inviting patrons to submit their own findings of "literary and musical roots." Add these to the display, which can be hung or placed on a table, using easel-frames.

Illus. 35 and 36 show classic wall arrangements to frame the library materials you want to show. Illus. 37 shows a possible wall and table arrangement, perhaps for books on flower-arranging, with an arrangement and a book for browsing.

Illus. 38 is for a single book. Both the book and the frame can be propped up on a stand. The card alongside simply says, "Frame Your Thoughts Through Reading." Choose a philosophical work to display.

You can put up a framed mirror, as in Illus. 39, and invite library volunteers, or use the prop for any other "picture yourself ..." (such as Picture Yourself on a Dangerous Mission) and place all those books that thrust the hero into precisely that kind of predicament on a nearby table.

Illus. 32. HINGED FRAMES FOR SERIES

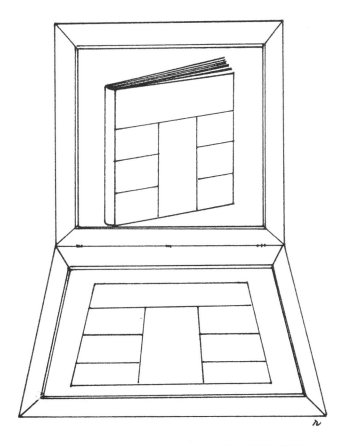

Illus. 33. HINGED FRAME FOR BOOKS AND RECORD

Illus. 34. GALLERY OF LIBRARY AND MUSICAL ANCESTORS

Illus. 35. CLASSIC ARRANGEMENTS

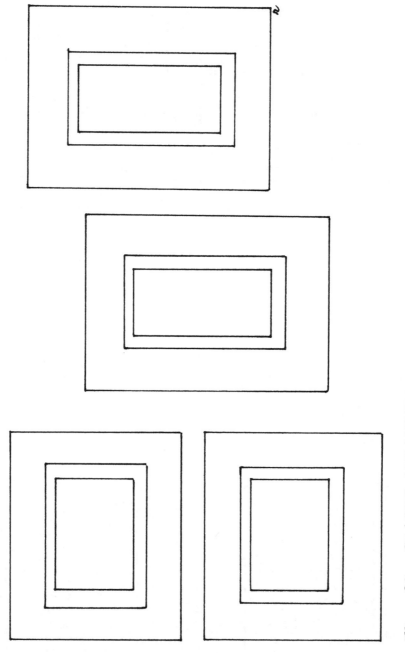

Illus. 36. CLASSIC ARRANGEMENTS

Illus. 37. WALL AND TABLE ARRANGEMENTS

Illus. 38.   FRAME YOUR THOUGHTS THROUGH READING

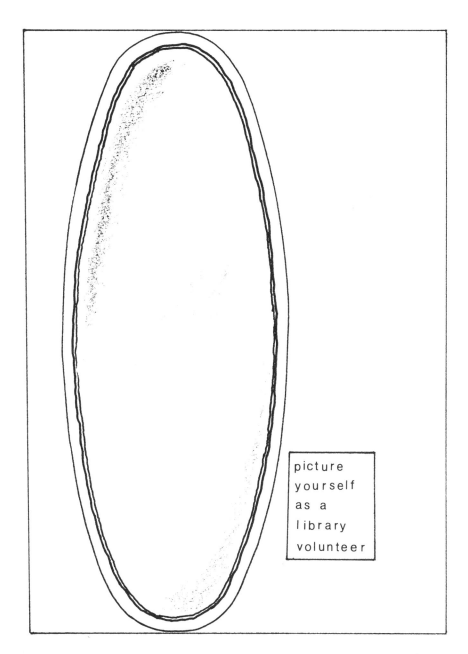

picture
yourself
as a
library
volunteer

Illus. 39. PICTURE YOURSELF AS A LIBRARY
VOLUNTEER

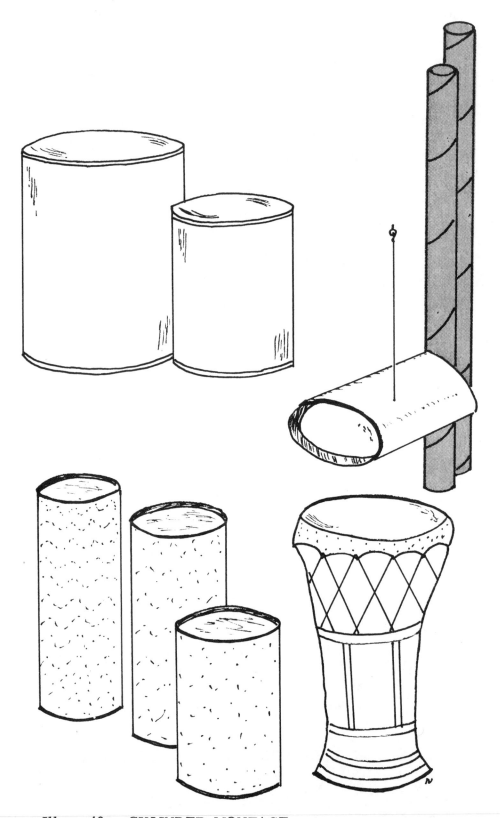

Illus. 40. CYLINDER MONTAGE

44

CYLINDERS

Objective of the display:

To feature traditional and nontraditional library materials in a dramatic manner, to communicate reports visually, and to utilize architectural aspects of the library (especially pillars).

Adjuncts to the display:

Comprehensive focus on PUPPETRY through:
1) shows performed for audiences in the library;
2) workshops in script-writing and puppet and puppet-stage construction;
3) seminars on puppetry, such as development of puppetry as an entertainment form, national traditions in puppetry, fantasy and reality, or "Pinocchio Revisited";
4) annotated and illustrated bibliographies (for various ages) of library materials on puppetry;
5) a series of newspaper features on uses of puppets available on loan from the library as teaching/learning devices in home and classroom settings.

Presentation of POSTERS as an art form through:
1) exhibit of posters with annotations regarding the style and artist (work done locally, a library-system traveling show, etc.);
2) workshops on poster design and production;
3) seminars on the elements of poster design, advertising and aesthetic aspects of posters, comparison of posters as national communicators;
4) simulating of the traditional European poster column (these free-standing items are commercially available in catalogs of library furnishings and equipment).

Presentation of SCULPTURE as an art form through:
1) exhibit, as for posters;
2) classes in beginning sculpture;

3) seminars or lectures on the history of sculpture or on the work of modern sculptors in relation to their predecessors.

Focus on CEREMONIAL EVENTS that evolve around poles (May dance, totem).

Spotlight on CYLINDERS through:
   1) a series on the uses of cylinders in industry, communication, architecture, medicine, scientific investigation, astronomy, music, games, toys;
   2) craft classes for fun and practical uses of cylinders (cans, containers, tubes).

Patron voting on favorite library materials in various categories.

Remember to arrange for media coverage for all of your special activities.

Discussion of the display:

Cylinders are marvelous display vehicles because of their availability, versatility, minimal cost, easy storage, and adaptability to endless moods, themes, and missions. Cylinders--such as tubes, cans, drums, pipes, pedestals, hassocks, buckets, and columns and posts within the library structure--can be utilized for both permanent and special displays, either as the focal point or as props or surfaces for displays on any number of topics. See "Exciting Interior Decor," pp. 114-131, Have You Got What They Want?, by Rita Kohn and Krysta Tepper (Metuchen, N.J.: Scarecrow, 1982), for a discussion on how school librarians can take advantage of columns and posts as the focal points of "centers."

Sturdy paper tubes of various diameters and lengths are available at little or no cost as throwaways from wallpaper, fabric, and printing shops. Hand-dip ice cream parlors and restaurants will save their reusable buckets, tubs, and oversized cans for the asking. Tennis players, homemakers, and everyone else will respond to a well-publicized plea for cylindrical containers and tubes of every size.

You can place cylinders on tables and on tops of low shelving, you can anchor them to the floor or have them be free-standing, you can suspend them from the ceiling, glue them together, use them vertically, horizontally, or at a rakish tilt (like the Leaning Tower of Pisa). They become pillars, posts, and poles, open-ended, one end open and one closed, totally encased. They can hold items on them, in them, between them, over them.

A display of cylinders can include such items as kaleidoscopes, telescopes, microscopes, binoculars, piston chambers, pipes (plumbing, drainage), musical instruments, medical instruments, household containers, models of silos, and anything else you can locate that falls into the shape. Naturally, you'll want to place the appropriate library materials alongside the real objects. A fun, hands-on display could be a small printing press that uses a cylinder for the inking process.

Puppets can be placed through tubes and cans and can be hung singly or in groups as a mobile. These approaches can be a fresh way to bring attention to much-loved puppets available for loan or for in-library use; or they can display new puppets made in library-sponsored workshops or in workshops elsewhere in the community, but put on public display in the library. (See Illus. 41.)

To let people know that a variety of tastes in library materials is quite a good thing, create a grouping of drums. (See Illus. 42.) Use the real things if someone has a few that are beyond musical use but nevertheless are still somewhat intact or are of the sturdy tribal variety; otherwise, you can turn tubs into drums. Add a sign that says, "Borrow to Your Own Drum Beat," and place on the drums items that are available. If there is a headless drum at hand, use it as a swap-shop for jobs wanted by young people. Put up a sign that announces, "Beat Your Own Drum" or "Advertise Your Skills." Have application forms available for the person to list name, how to be reached, what kind of work is desired, credentials for doing that work, and the range of pay expected.

Illus. 43 shows a display that draws attention to patron voting for library materials that are special enough to be put up on a pedestal (Illus. 44). Illus. 43 gets its rakish tilt from cylinders pushed into styrofoam at an angle. Tennis-ball containers make good ballot-holders; cans that once held fruits, vegetables, or soups can be converted into attractive pencil and blank-ballot containers.

Traditionally, a pedestal has three parts: base, midsection, and cap. Pedestals can be made by anchoring tubs or cans of one size into styrofoam bases that are somewhat larger and then capping the midsection with a lid or can with a larger circumference. Marbleized paper can complete the "stereotyped" look. The sign can read: "YOUR CHOICES: UP ON A PEDESTAL!" Arrange the voting or survey procedure for wide exposure and general fun. Then, when the ballots or surveys are in for each particular time period and category, place the "winners" on the pedestals. Use an accompanying display of runners-up and supply a short bibliography or annotation, if appropriate, for your library situation. Run a series of news stories on the "Pedestal Placers."

Pedestals can also be used to display artwork by local residents or to display sculpture available on loan from the library. Varying the sizes and heights of pedestals adds to their effectiveness. You might even be able to assemble several authentic period pedestals and feature them along with the items they hold up.

Other vertical uses of cylinders are pictured in Illus. 45. Group cylinders as needed for a specific purpose. Sketch "a" shows cylinders arranged in bar-graph fashion. With lengths ruled off accordingly, you can provide annual-report data, including circulation figures and numbers of card-holders in categories of age, in quadrants of the community, or in comparison with the total population. Cylinders, like a bar graph, can also indicate budget expenditures for the year and can be saved to provide a comparative display for next year. Each tube can be identified directly on its surface or by a legend adhered to the surface upon which the 3-D bar graph is placed.

If space factors dictate a vertical arrangement for a 3-D bar graph, utilize the capability in that way. Another way to show statistics is via cylinders that will hold the library item ("d"); e. g., film circulation 10% of total, book circulation 78. 6% of total, magazine circulation 3% of total.

The other four sketches show different kinds of groupings. You can cover cylinders with fabric or paper to create moods and images, depending upon the materials you want to display and the effect you want to create. As with sketch "b," you can change display surfaces by adding another element to the top of a cylinder. Sketch "c" is a grouping that has been glued together to be free-standing for the display of smaller objects (perhaps toys or miniature art pieces made by patrons in a library art program). A trio of tall cylinders ("e") or a quintet of short cylinders ("f") holds any number of items in almost any location within the library.

Illus. 46 demonstrates a potpourri of possibilities for displaying posters. Sketch "a" shows that you can glue tubes together and hang them, by sturdy cord or wire, from a rod. You can hang an open poster on both sides of the glued-together tubes that hold posters.

For a tabletop or shelf-top arrangement with different-sized tubes, "b" becomes an interesting pattern. Sketch "c" utilizes cylinders as containers, with a cloth rectangle as the display component for "Piles of Posters" slung from a hook on pegboard. The recently designed storage units of mesh quadrants ("f") can also easily hold rolls of posters, and a lot of other things, including puppets, just as you would use pegboard for a puppet-display surface.

Build an attractive display area ("d") by anchoring two or more sturdy tubes in a sturdy base (such as cement blocks). Items of high interest can be pinned up between "poles." Thus, when you build this item, measure the distance between tubes to be right for whatever it is you will want to hang. It can be for notices of upcoming events or of special materials available for borrowing.

Items that need to be stored vertically can be placed within a larger cylinder, as with the three tubes illustrated in "g." Such a combination can also be turned into a pedestal, with a cap that serves as a surface upon which to place objects.

Sketches "h" and "e" show two other ways to glue tubes together for display and container purposes. In both cases, the sides serve as surfaces for hanging things.

Sketch "i" demonstrates how to turn a rectangle into a cylinder. Merely fasten the edges together securely and, presto, you turn a two-dimensional item into a three-dimensional tool.

Maps, documents, clippings, letters, and so on can be exchanged for posters, consistently alluded to in this discussion. In fact, you can be as creative as you want to be in turning the idea of cylinders into an all-out display possibility.

Invite patrons to turn tubes into rockets, contraptions, castles, towers--anything at all--and give prizes for the most inventive, the sturdiest, the tallest, the most comical. Pull out books on pertinent topics. The library can invite teams of three to six people to bring cardboard tubes, masking tape, twine, paper clips, and magazines OK to tear up. They can have as much fun as the people pictured in Illus. 47 had during a session on the campus of Illinois State University in Normal. The photos are from a Management Training Seminar on "Building an Effective Work Team."

Illus. 48 points out a quartet of other inventive uses of cylinders. Turn an open-ended can into a holder for newspapers and magazines that are rolled up ("c"). Tip over a tub or a canister and let paperbacks spill out onto a tabletop ("b"). Mount a cylinder on a pole or hang it from the end of a bookshelf, from a column that is part of the library structure, or from a wall. Affix (with string, tape, or rubber bands) colored cellophane or plastic squares over one end of a cylinder (such as a coffee can or oatmeal box) and add a sign, "SPOTLIGHT ON _____," to draw attention to specific items ("a").

Ever since Oscar the Grouch made a garbage can "home," the lowly cylinder has gained class. Affix a sign that proclaims, "TRASH TO YOU IS TREASURE TO ME," and turn the garbage can into a free swap-shop ("d").

Pull out your gardening and house-plant collection of materials to show how to make an old soup can sprout parsley. Encourage a "cutting exchange" for people who bring one cutting and take another. (Glass cylinders are fine for rooting cuttings.) Illus. 49 provides one display possibility to combine gardening and crafts books, magazines, and pamphlets (and some fun!). The three-sided screen can fit over a table or in a case.

Take a page out of the traditional Tinker Toy pattern book and create displays from a combination of cylinders and rods ("a," "b," "c," and "d" of Illus. 50). Since knitting needles are a good linking item in this case, the combination of wool crafts works well. Not only can you show off knitted items, but such handcrafted things as yarn dolls as well. Sketch "e" shows useful items from cylinders. More are available from craft books. Sprinkle them around the table with this molecular-type display.

Of course, you can use "real things" for the display attraction to feature your library's collection. Paint cans, rollers, wallpaper, and a host of other "home improvement" products come in cylindrical shapes (such as caulking and adhesive products and rolls of linoleum, carpeting, building insulation, and roofing). Arrange them with your books, pamphlets, and periodicals on home improvement and building. Otherwise, have a paint or hardware store incorporate the library's home-improvement items in its display of merchandise. (See Illus. 51.)

To bring attention to a pattern exchange, create a display with bolts of cloth, spools and spindles of thread, and other sewing notions. Pin patterns to a cylinder and add an eye-catching caption, such as "SEW EASY," with the letters cut out with pinking shears. Illus. 52 is sketched for use in a window or in a case so that the bolts can't be knocked over and the fabric can be pinned to a wall.

Illus. 53 shows how to arrange "real objects" to advertise a library program. You can compose the data on information cards to spark extra interest. Because of the nature of the items, this display could best be mounted in a window or a case.

If your library has columns, take advantage of this architectural feature by building a seat around them--low seats for youngsters, higher seats for grown-ups. (See sketch "a" in Illus. 54.) Or be a bit fancier and construct a gazebo (as in "b" of Illus. 54).

Illus. 55 suggests a cylinder by outlining a circle on a glass surface and blocking out the area beyond the outer edge of the circumference. The display, placed in the case or window, appears to the viewer to be inside a cylinder. For this purpose, a raked platform ("a") can be most effective. This is easily built by placing a piece of board over several triangular wedges. Cover the board with a cloth covering that is appropriate and versatile (flannel, burlap, felt). This raked platform can easily be removed from the window or case (and stored or used elsewhere) when the flat bottom of the area is better for another display.

A step platform is another alternative to the flat-bottom area. Sketch "b" shows two sections that provide you with a capacity to build a display so that the items in back are easily visible over the items in front. These platforms or "risers" are also easy to construct from several rectangular blocks over which a top and a side board are nailed. These platforms can also be covered with fabric. You can choose diverse, but compatible, colors or use only a uniform, neutral shade.

We've been talking about cylinders for pages and still haven't exhausted all of the possibilities. You will think of constructing miniature rafts, "log cabins," may poles, totem poles, flag poles, water towers, or silos, to capture local interest and local activities and to tie them into what is available for everyone who cares to visit the library.

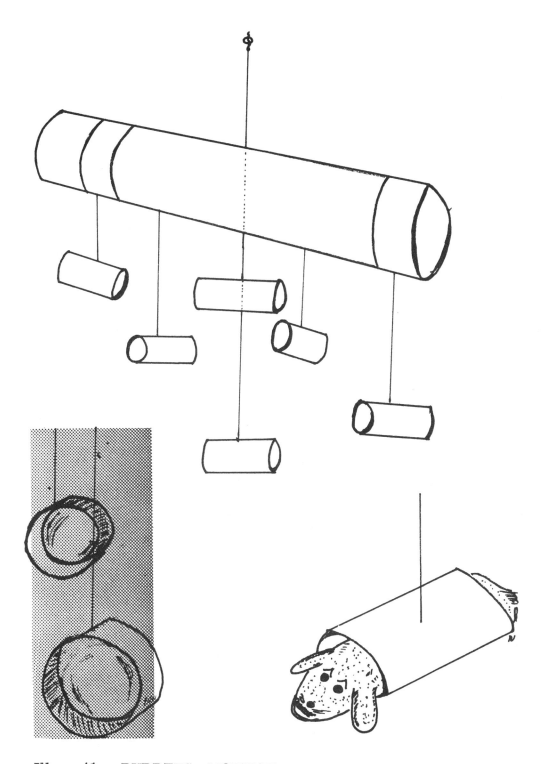

Illus. 41.   PUPPETS, MOBILES

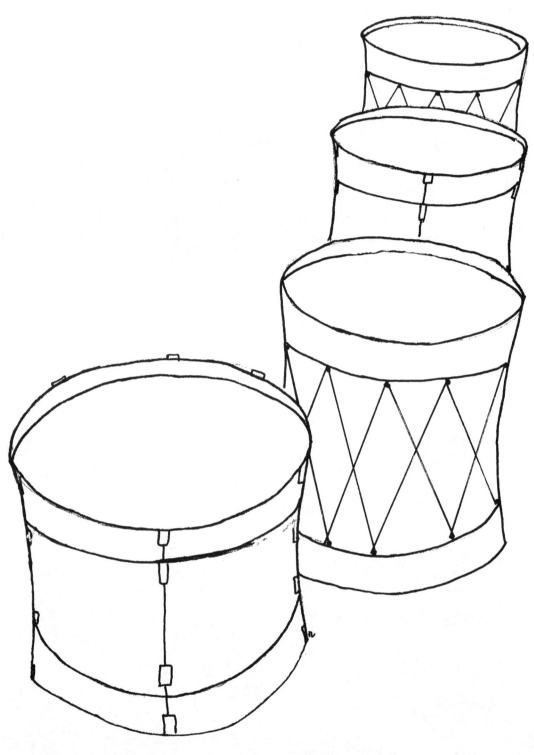

Illus. 42.   DRUMS

Illus. 43.   PEDESTAL PLACER NOMINATIONS

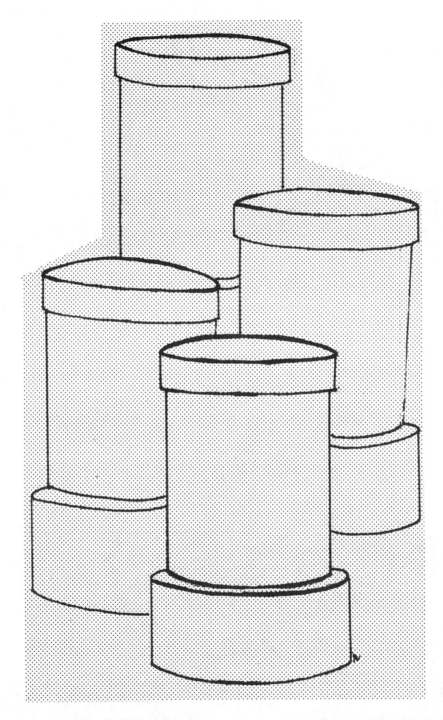

Illus. 44. PEDESTALS

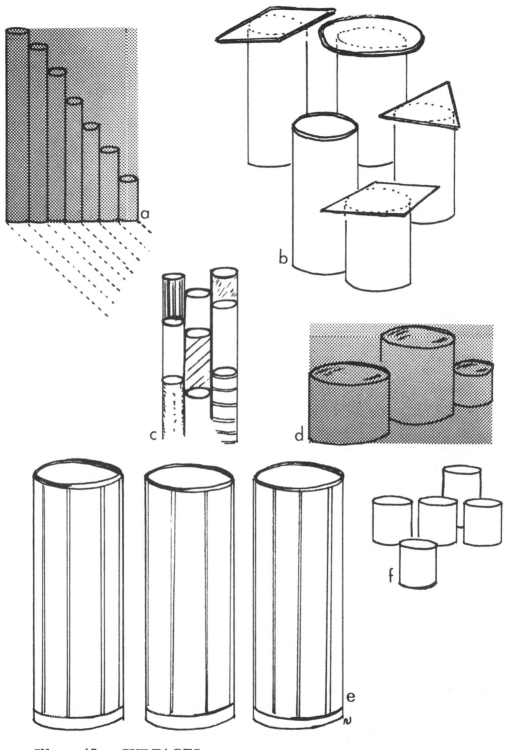

Illus. 45. SURFACES

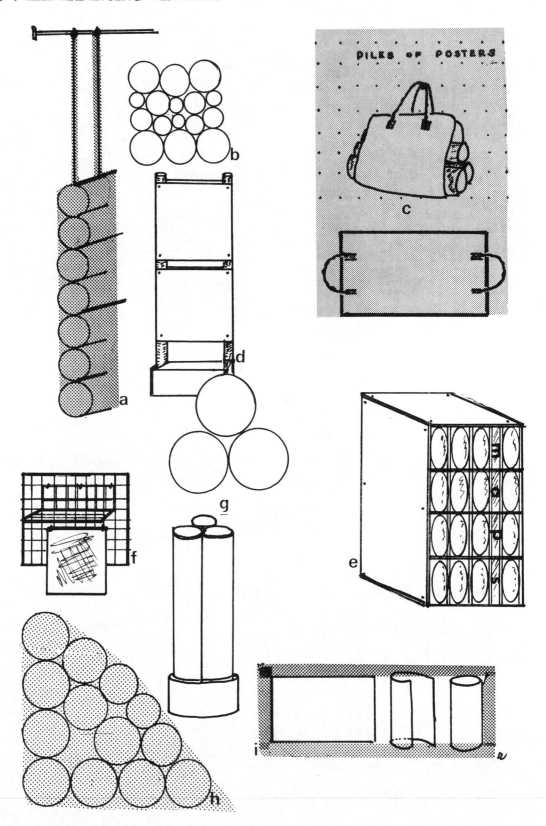

Illus. 46.   TUBES

Illus. 47. PHOTOS OF CREATIVE TUBING

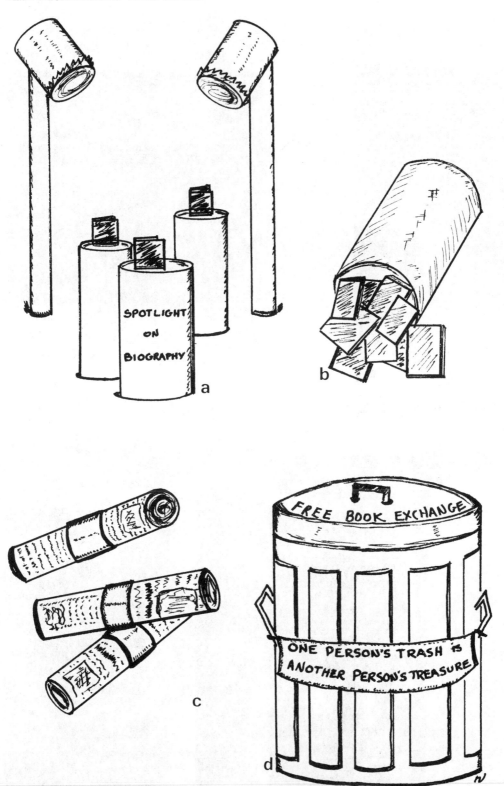

Illus. 48. TRASH CAN, SPOTLIGHT, NAPKIN RING

Illus. 49.   GARDENING

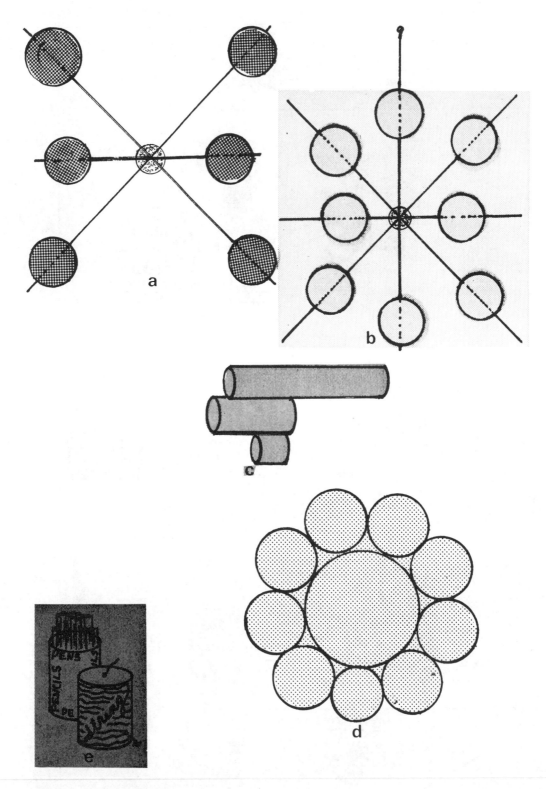

Illus. 50.   "TINKER TOY"

Illus. 51.   IMPROVEMENT BEGINS AT HOME

Illus. 52. IT'S SEW EASY

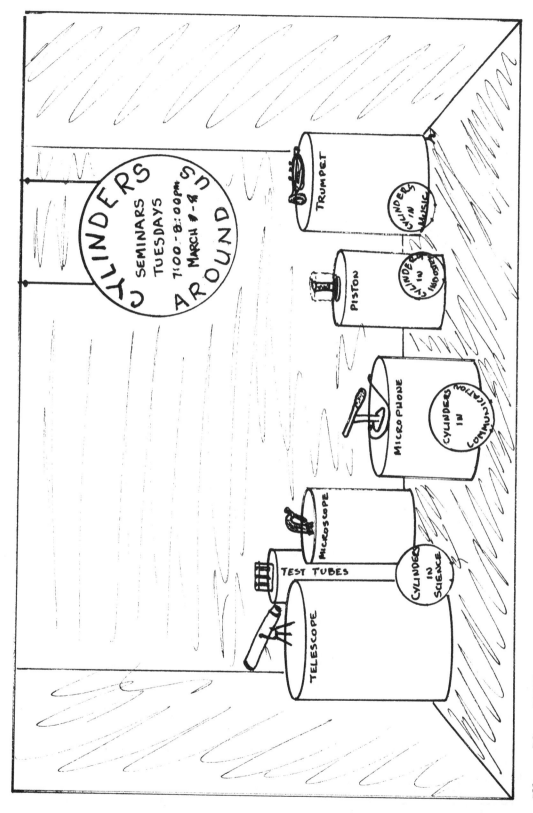

Illus. 53. CYLINDERS AROUND US

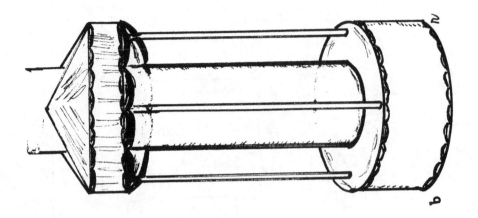

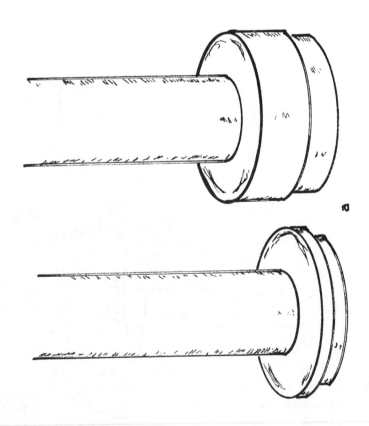

Illus. 54.   UTILIZE ARCHITECTURE

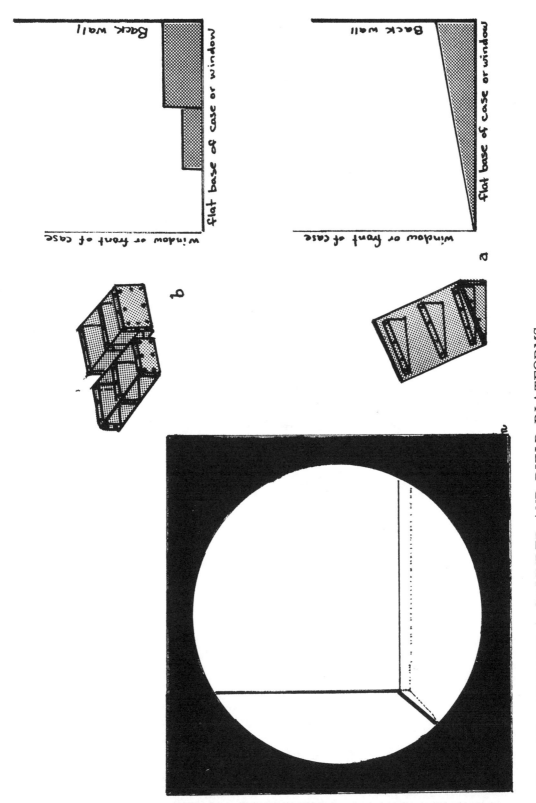

Illus. 55. CREATE A CYLINDER AND BUILD PLATFORMS

Illus. 56.   THE PERFECT SETTING

TABLE SETTINGS

_____

Objective of the display:

Showing off everything possible in your collection, this display idea is particularly well suited to providing library-use training and library-materials introduction for a variety of publics.

Adjuncts to the display:

1) Working with the theme of "We serve all tastes" or "We cater to everyone," you can design informational materials (in the form of menus) on all genres of literature and on all styles of music, filmmaking, and theater. One approach is to acquire a sample menu from eating establishments (of every kind) in your area and beyond, to use as a model for your own "menu-making." Illus. 57 shows two possibilities, both pinned up wherever they can attract attention (on a post, on an end of shelving, etc.). Sketch "a" is informative, "b" is a teaser. As an accompaniment to the theme, a series of seminars can be presented on such topics as "Mastery of Mystery," "Fine Art of Fiction," "Meandering Through Mythology," "High Hopes in Heroes," "Pursuing the Poet," "The Range of Realism," or "Beguiling Biographies." Carry the menu concept one step further to advertise "specials of the day" or "specials of the week" and announce events in and out of the library. It is usually better to advertise a category rather than one specific title so as not to run out after "the first order."

2) Run a series on linking literature with living for parents of the young child (and for parents-to-be). "We Cater to Carry-Outs" (to help parents "carry out" their desired reading plans with their children) can be an umbrella title for topics that include:
a) creating a home environment for reading,
b) the foundation of nursery rhymes and folk literature during infancy,
c) library visits and reading aloud with the toddler,
d) choosing books with the emerging reader, and
e) maintaining the reading habit in the middle years.

3) "A la Carte" can be an opportunity for people to plug into programs of individual value regarding the use of specific library skills and techniques. Examples are a basic introduction to the collection of the library for new patrons, investigation of reference tools (including computerized materials), or research methods in the electronic age. You can announce all of the programs on an "A la Carte" menu and have people "order" the ones they want to attend--one, some, or all. Sign-up for each session can be on a pad, as for a food order. (See Illus. 58.)

4) "Recipes for Relaxin' " provides a format for introducing individual titles within genres in the print and nonprint collections. This is a good opportunity for parading out the older titles along with the more recent acquisitions.

5) A program on the art and components of table setting, historically and for present-day daily and entertaining use can run throughout the length of the display feature. See Illus. 59 for an announcement idea.

6) "Reading Recipe Roundup," an exchange of ideas on how to introduce reluctant readers to books, is a possibility for an informal session among teachers, parents, and librarians. Books, ideas, and programs, as well as problems and frustrations, can be shared, but the emphasis is on enjoying a balanced diet of reading materials.

7) "Vintage Authors" is a motivation for examining the books of authors who have been reappearing on library shelves and who seem to improve with longevity. This also can be an opportune time to investigate the trends of "debunking" by critics of authors. (See Illus. 60.)

Discussion of the display:

Table settings have been known to draw people to homes across a community as a fund-raising activity. You can turn the library into a tour of table settings within all of the departments. You can do it up straight, with lovely settings utilizing the expertise of individuals and retailers, or you can use the settings as a prop to display library materials, or you can combine the two options with a month-long theme of "table settings" in the library.

For the real settings, develop a title to coincide with the season or a community event, such as "Settings for Summer" or "Centennial Suppers, Breakfasts, and Lunches." Bring in tables or use those cylinders as an alternative to tabletops for display surfaces. If you are bringing in very lovely and valuable pieces, either as centerpieces or as flatware and dishes, you may want to consider using only your glass cases, or plastic domes that seal to protect the borrowed items.

Employing the concepts of fork, knife, spoon, and plate in the other direction, you can place-set the utensils with library materials on the plates or on side dishes. The title cards can tell the story: "Food for Thought," "Books Are Your Just Desserts," "Classic Specialities of the House," "Brace of Best-Sellers," "Novel Ingredients," "Continental Cuisine." See Illus. 61 and 62 as examples.

It's fun to "set places" with a book, record, or film and to stack a bunch of other items nearby, with the legend: "You're welcome to seconds, thirds, fourths ... " or "Give Yourself a Break. " (See Illus. 63 and 64.)

Make up trays for special occasions or needs. "Breakfast in Bed" can sport a rolled-up magazine; "Miserable with the Mumps?" can be complemented by a fantasy title for the age group that's into the contagious disease that season; "Saturday in the Sun" might be a good time to slide in some science fiction, gothics, or sports biographies. You get the idea! See Illus. 65 for one way to handle it.

A possibility for featuring a play is to count up the parts and to bill it as "Service for Seven" (or whatever the number of characters; see Illus. 66).

Borrow a line from the poetry of Ben Jonson and alter it somewhat to say, "Drink to Us Only with Your Eyes ... and Ears. " Illus. 67 suggests one way to make this point.

If alcoholic beverages are an OK thing in your community, you can work in a number of meaningful analogies. Illus. 68 singles out books, but you can substitute records, films, tapes, or magazines for a full listing of items to be enjoyed.

Illus. 69 is a possibility for working in very limited space. Try such displays in a dozen spots throughout the library. Constantly replace library materials that are borrowed. Of course, you'll not want to use valuable flatware as the display props. "Dig In" can be effected with plastic throwaways or old forks, knives, and spoons picked up at group sales.

Illus. 70 is a sketch of what a patron can see when entering the adult area. A series of tables can feature a changing variety of offerings. In this sketch, the table in the foreground sports a sign that reads: "Fiction for Two. " The next table is a "Biography Buffet. " Beyond that, the sign reads, "Reserved" (for books on reserve!). "Tape and Platter" is the announcement on the table in the background. The offerings are recordings and cassette and eight-track tapes along with talking-book materials.

This theme can be utilized for bulletin-board space by adding a placemat or a cloth as the background and by using book jackets that are appropriate to the topic, as per the messages above and phrases you think of on your own.

Hanging displays will work, too, with a placemat, paper plate, and plastic flatware as the background upon which to hang book jackets. You should think in terms of using both sides of the placemat for such a hanging display. You can add any number of titles as an eye-catching device, along with having placemats swaying overhead at varying heights--on sturdy wire or twine, of course! (See Illus. 71.)

If you've enjoyed the foregoing appetizer on the table setting theme, just think of the pleasure you'll experience dishing up some delicious main ideas on your own. Bon appétit--and happy munching--as long as you don't have to eat your own words (shades of The Phantom Tollbooth and Alice in Wonderland).

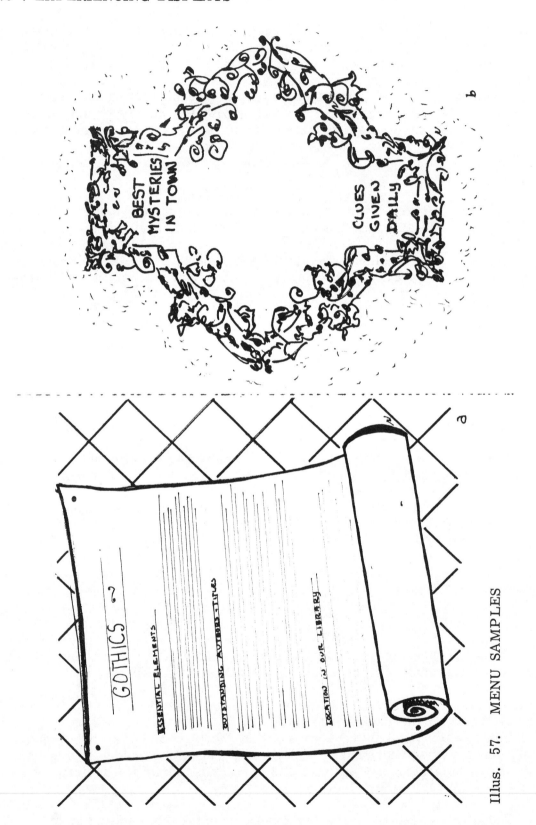

Illus. 57. MENU SAMPLES

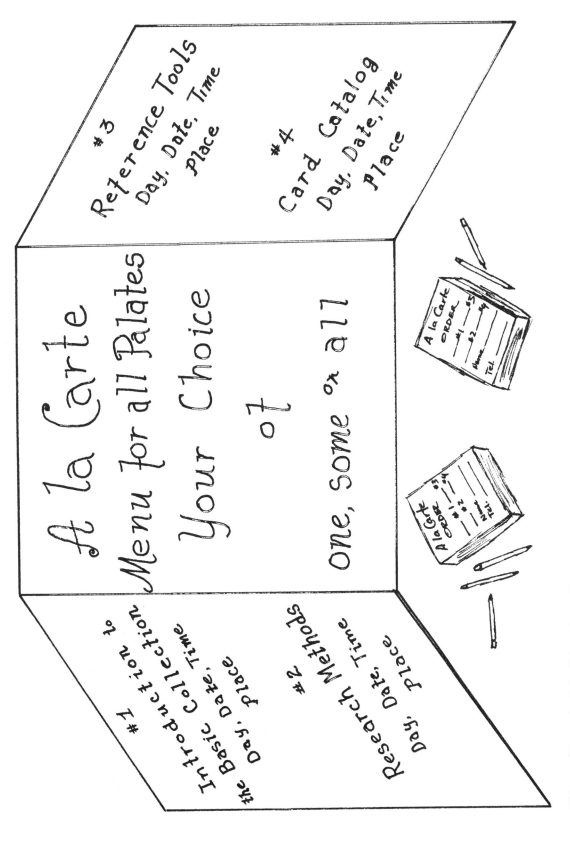

Illus. 58. A LA CARTE MENUS

TABLE SETTINGS THROUGH THE AGES

SUNDAY MAY 21, 1984
2:00 PM

Illus. 59. TABLE SETTINGS THROUGH THE AGES

Illus. 60.   VINTAGE AUTHORS

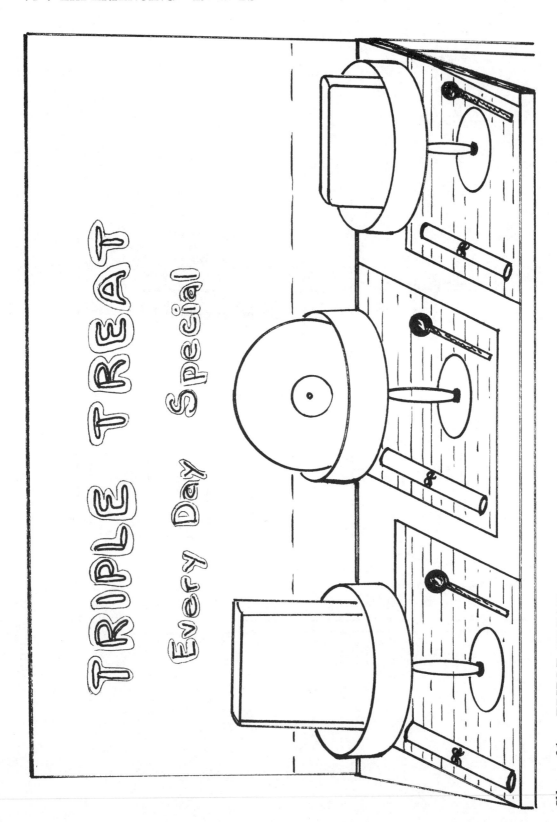

Illus. 61.   TRIPLE TREAT

Illus. 63.   HELP YOURSELF TO SECONDS AND THIRDS

Illus. 62.   THE PROOF OF THE PLOT IS IN THE READING

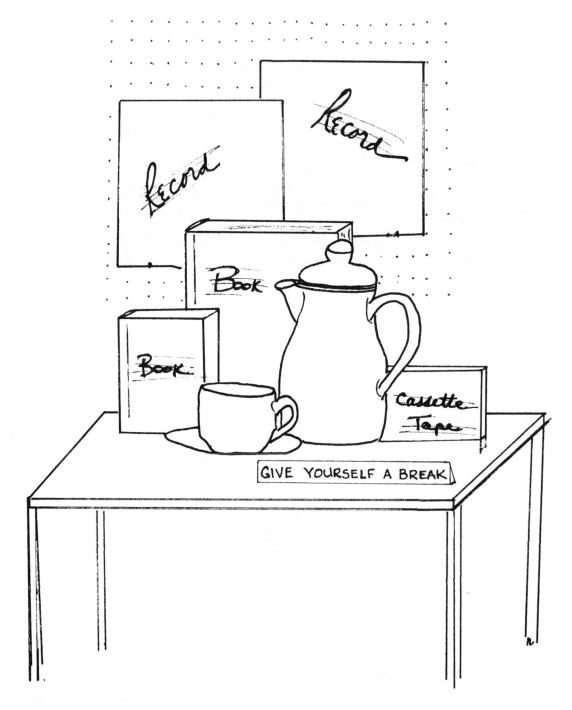

Illus. 64.   GIVE YOURSELF A BREAK

Illus. 65. BEDTIME TREAT

Illus. 66.   SERVICE FOR SEVEN OR ...

Illus. 67.   DRINK TO US ONLY WITH YOUR EYES ... AND EARS

Illus. 68. BOOKS ON THE ROCKS, VINTAGE ENJOYMENT

Illus. 69. DIG IN!

Illus. 70.   TABLE SETTINGS

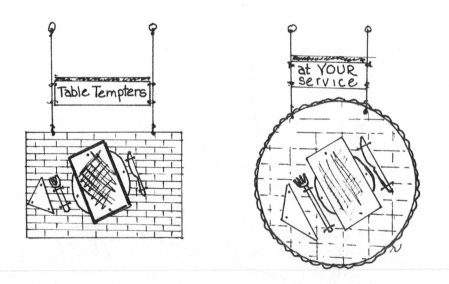

Illus. 71.   TABLE TEMPTERS, AND AT YOUR SERVICE

PEOPLE

Objective of the display:

To introduce people all the way around: people who are connected with the library--board, staff, patrons, benefactors; people in the community generally--elected and appointed officials, civic leaders, public servants (paid and volunteer, business people, industrialists, inventors, artists, musicians, doctors, writers, dancers, actors, athletes, children, teens, adults); people in the books in the library--fiction and nonfiction.

To illustrate how the library makes a difference in the lives of people.

To revive the valid theme that "The Library Is the PEOPLE Place."

Adjuncts to the display:

1) Plan activities by the people, for the people, of the people. Start with the founding documents of the United States of America. Along with the display of the documents and a pictorial-biographical exhibit of the leading personalities of the eighteenth-century "birth of New World democracy," set up a series of town meetings, lectures, and discussion groups on the act of governing and the art of citizen participation in all levels of government in your area today.

2) Develop an oral-history project based on occupations, historical events, social movements, personal vignettes, or whatever is relevant to your area.

3) Provide workshops in genealogical research and preservation of family records and documents.

4) Organize a career day with provisions for adult re-entry along with career pursuits for high school students.

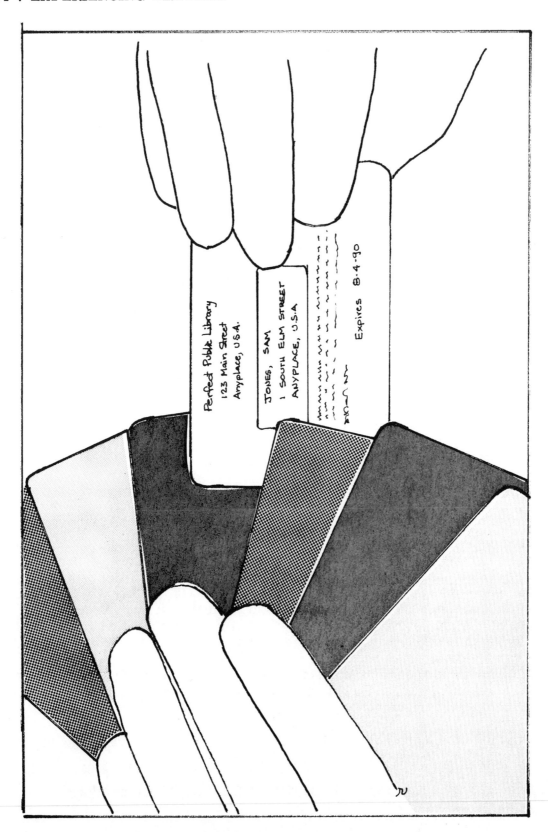

Illus. 72.   PICK THE PERFECT CARD

5) Set up a series on characterization in fiction and development of personalities in biographical research and writing.

6) Feature interests of people in your area, be it their hobbies, avocations, vocations, or passions. Have them share those interests during an "Interest Fair. "

7) Capitalize on any distinctive national groups in your area by setting up "Community Days" with foods, dress, crafts, and customs that are indigenous to the people of that group.

8) Show how people communicate with each other: letter-writing as an art in friendship, how direct dialing happens as a feat of technology, the making of greeting cards for all occasions, sign language, body language, advertising, the news media, tapes sent in lieu of letters.

9) Arrange an open house at the library where patrons and staff and board members can meet each other socially without conducting library business.

10) Set up "Patron of the Day" or "Staff Member of the Day" by selecting people at random ahead of time, getting a brief biography, presenting each with a flower (women and men) and arranging for media coverage.

11) Set up a videotaping operation so that people can see themselves in action at the library--either to air an opinion, to recommend or pan a piece of writing, film, recording, or artwork, or to present an original sketch or reading.

12) Promote a project that is people-oriented and that will be of lasting value in your area--a park, an annual storytelling festival, or a student exchange program. You'll know what is right for your particular situation.

13) Initiate a series of monthly lectures on the care and feeding of the human being or on "the seven ages of humankind. "

14) Arrange a community-organization week so that representatives of each group can have time and space to tell and show what it does. New members can sign up or projects can be promoted, and so on.

15) Have a program on "Standard Stereotypes: The Good and the Bad" and invite discussion groups.

16) Have a program on "portraiture on Canvas and Film. "

17) Have a program on the making of documentaries.

18) Have a program on "Heroes" and another on "Debunking: Everyone Is Eligible. "

19) Set up an all-day seminar on "Options over 60" with a panel of people who have planned retirement and are in it. Have economists, bankers,

lawyers, sociologists, or psychologists give practical and honest advice about retirement-planning. Have children of people who have retired or are planning retirement on a panel to discuss how they, the children, feel about their parents' retirement. Have owners of "retirement complexes" describe what is involved in the purchase of living space in such a specially designed living area.

20) Set up a lecture series on "Emotions: How to Know Them, How to Show Them. "

Discussion of the display:

The concept of "People," as a set of visual elements, can be built into a display in any number of ways, including through photographs, line drawings, caricatures, cartoons, collages, sketches, silhouettes, papier-mâché figures, mannequins, stuffed clothing, or wire figures. "People" can also be implied --for instance, by placing props in a way that intimates that people are present, or by picturing hands (as with line drawings or with gloves) or eyes, or by using glasses, shoes, masks, or special uniforms, among many other possibilities.

One stylistic aim in the display ideas that follow is to utilize the usual library-display facilities in a dramatic manner. Hence, patrons can see larger-than-life (or life-sized) cutouts of people (see Illus. 73) placed within glass cases. Outlines of people can be cut from cardboard packing boxes. After painting the figures a color appropriate to the display, tack the end figures to a flat surface (pillars, a wall, or two sturdy panels) and permit the middle figures to arch out, giving a strikingly dimensional effect. Of course, you can be as artistic or as whimsical as you want and paint on faces and clothing or glue on cloth that is cut as clothing.

The glass cases can feature the hobbies or collectibles of patrons, memorabilia from the past, significant and rare documents, items relating to customs of a national group, and so on.

Illus. 74 gives a twist to the familiar. Here is a large-sized silhouette of an easily recognized profile, placed on a screen, bulletin board, or wall. Cut-up logs, something freely associated with Abraham Lincoln, are good for holding library materials on or about Lincoln, his period in history, and figures associated with him. Feature the library's tape of someone reciting the "Gettysburg Address" along with a framed copy of the document. Have available a list of any films available that deal with Lincoln, his presidency, and the Civil War.

Illus. 75 is one way to present the people currently in Washington, D.C. The line-art background clearly identifies the location. You can get a photograph and biographical data on each individual and a brief description of each cabinet post by writing to the Office of the President, Washington, D.C. 20006. Even though the descriptions of the Presidency and Vice-Presidency are contained in the U.S. Constitution (a copy of which you can put on display), you should request data on these offices, too, along with photos and biographies of these two officeholders. Material on senators and representatives is available from their offices in either Washington, D.C., or at their local addresses. When writing, explain why you want the material and offer to send a photo of the completed display. Of course, invite your senators and representatives to visit your library to view the display and perhaps also to be a program participant. You can follow a similar format for state, county, and local officeholders. Add your library materials pertinent to the subject, especially newspapers, newsmagazines, and recently published books on the Washington scene and on Capital personalities. You might also want to itemize pending bills or recently passed legislation of consequence to your area.

Set up a spot (Illus. 76) to tell folks about their very own library board, staff, friends, and volunteers, as well as all sorts of other local people. If someone on your staff is good at sketching, use sketches. Otherwise, formal photos or candid snapshots do very nicely. When spotlighting library personnel, place related materials nearby, including a copy of the library's bylaws, American Library Association acquisition guidelines, professional library literature (journals and books), membership blanks to join the friends-of-the-library organization, forms for running (or showing interest in being appointed) for a position on the library board, and forms to register as a library volunteer.

Let's take a few minutes to discuss surfaces for this display, other than glass cases (used in Illus. 73). Illus. 77 shows a variety of possibilities for movable bulletin boards and screens. Portable steps are very useful as display surfaces. The sketch shows a complete three-step unit. Graduated risers in sections work well, too. This arrangement has greater flexibility than does the single unit, but it won't be as sturdy if you invite young children to climb or sit.

Illus. 78 shows five other surfaces. Sketch "a" combines a novelty screen with a platform; "b" is a six-panel screen that can be used on both sides; "c" is a placard-and-easel combination for attracting attention to shelves and cases; "d" is standard display equipment in retail stores, with a lot of nice potential in a library setting; "e" creates a different kind of display space by placing together two tables of different heights.

Illus. 79 indicates another way to put cutout figures to work. In "a," slip a magazine of interest to the house-painter under one arm (cut out slits the right size for the magazine). While this hand has a drawn-on bucket, the other hand can be holding a library bag. The bag can fit over a mitten-type hand that is turned up with sculpture wire. This kind of figure can also stand on a fixture, like the one in sketch "b." You can rig up a hanger-hook to hold the library bag. Figure "c" is another silhouette, with a bit of whimsy. It's a fun way to attract attention to materials of opinion, or to draw attention to a spot where opinions can be voiced.

Illus. 80 utilizes cartoon art to draw attention to an opinion corner that emphasizes positive responses. The items that "everyone is raving about" can be library-related materials, services and programs, or a play in progress at the local theater, a film currently showing, an exhibit at the community center, a menu item at a nearby restaurant, and so on. People can share their enthusiasm on a card or a slip of paper and pin it up for all to see. Have the card or paper blank or be a bit fancy by creating something with a border and an easy fill-in format. What follows is a possibility:

I'M RAVING ABOUT:

_____

_____

_____

BECAUSE:_____

_____

_____

_____
signed

_____
date

Place these blanks in a pocket, with pencils available, and pin the pocket to the lower corner of the display.

Illus. 81 and 82 are suggestions for away-from-the-library displays. Illus. 81 can be a poster or a closed case display of photographs of people in the act of reading, listening to, or viewing library materials while at home, at the beach, in the park. The mannequins in Illus. 82 can be holding a library book and a library bag in a front window or in an in-store display. The message can be subtle, permitting the book and bag to tell their story on their own; or a title card, placed near the figures, can give pertinent data about library hours, address, and telephone number.

Masks work well for materials that are of a psychological or theatrical bent. Try something different with how you stack books for display. Illus. 83 shows one way that could work nicely for a window display.

Illus. 84, 85, and 86 are made up of "real" items that work well in a library for topical materials. Illus. 84 introduces a variety of possibilities for a time of relaxation. Illus. 85 is fine for pulling out general sports materials, and Illus. 81 pinpoints a specialized area. The uniform can be posed with sculpture wire and held up with a stand or pinned on a display surface, such as "a" of Illus. 79. The books on the martial arts can be set out around the platform.

Other "real" props to use in a display setup include gardening tools, rolls of architectural drawings, or guitars to complement aspects in your collection. Shoes work well, too. A great deal can be suggested with work boots, fishing boots, drum-major boots, track shoes, wing tips, ballet slippers, or high heels. You'll have lots of fun being creative with this possibility.

Illus. 72 introduced this section. You can use a variety of headlines, such as "you'll go wild with this card," "The pick of any deck," or get directly to the point with "Go ahead, use it ... you've paid for it through taxes," if you are putting the display up outside of the library where a lot of nonusers can see it.

Hand it to 'em with Illus. 87. Pile or pin up an example of every kind of item available with that "unbelievably useful" card. You should also put up a networking map and show what's available through interlibrary loan. Of course, you don't need to be told what to spread out for this display. If you draw the hand, cut a slit around the thumb to fit in a library card. Otherwise, give shape to a glove, using sculpture wire. Illus. 88 is another possibility for a similar message.

Illus. 89 is a tracing of an adult hand. It's dramatic alone, but when used within other settings a hand can provide a definite message, as in Illus. 90 and 91. Illus. 90 makes a good background for a historic display. Illus. 91 goes well with recordings on display.

Put gloves around propped-up books or shape cutout paper hands around them. A very attractive tabletop or bulletin-board display can be built from a variety of gloves or cutout hands placed around book jackets (for the bulletin board) or around books (for tabletops). (See Illus. 92.)

Hands of children, in different poses with books, make for an attractive frame around a bulletin board of book jackets, as in Illus. 93. Either line drawings or pinned yarn do well here.

You'll no sooner finish reading this than you'll begin to observe people and create displays that reflect their activities, interests, and needs, with them as the focal point. Does all this seem to click? Then enjoy, and gradually join me for the next section!

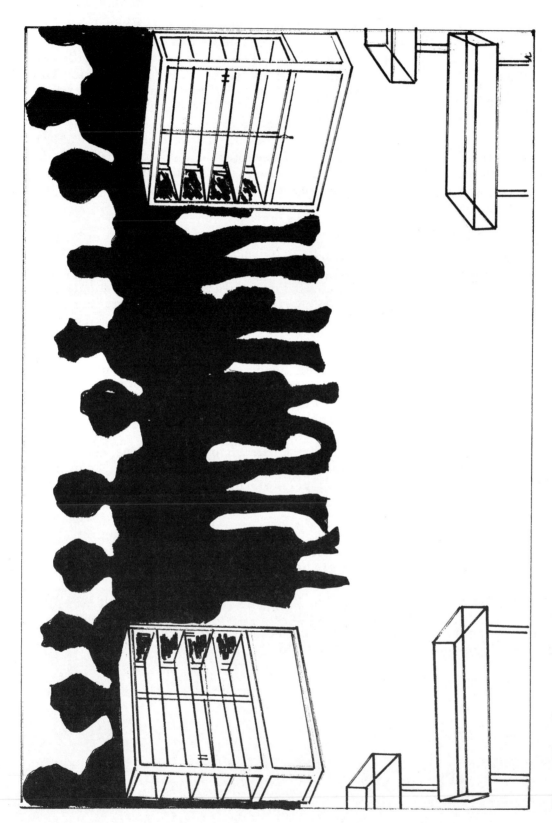

Illus. 73. CUTOUTS AND CASES

Illus. 74.   ABRAHAM LINCOLN

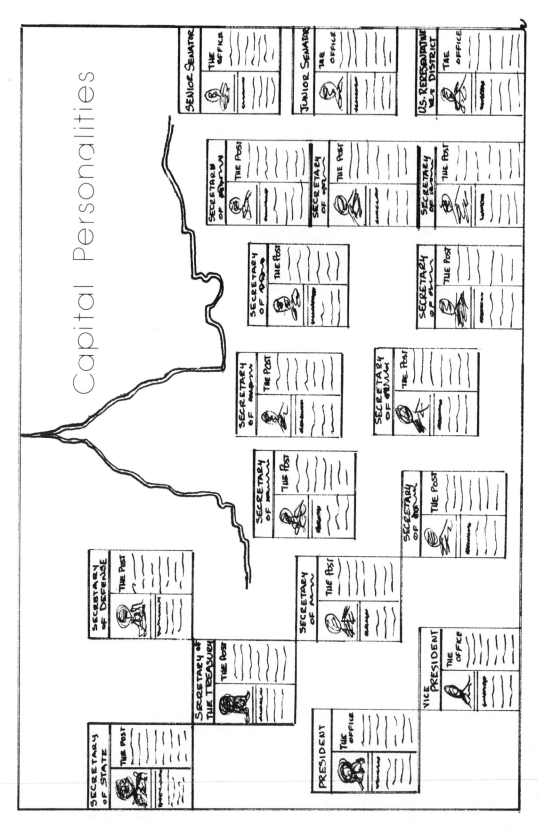

Illus. 75. CAPITAL PERSONALITIES

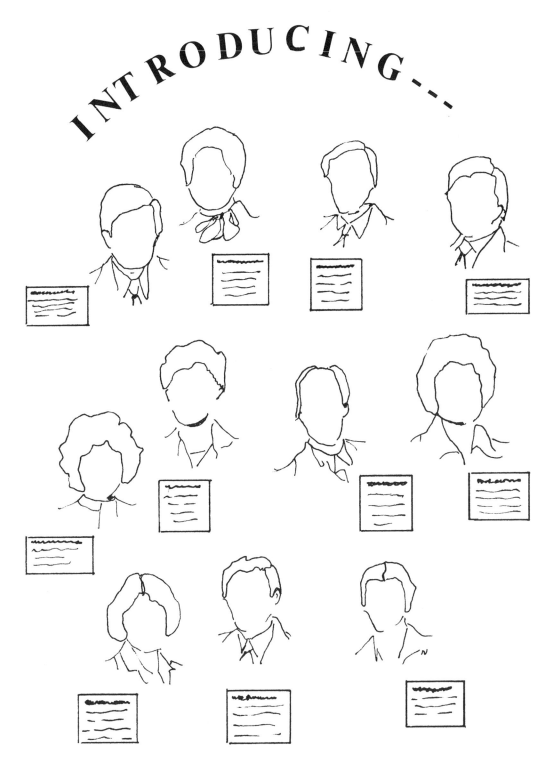

Illus. 76.   INTRODUCING

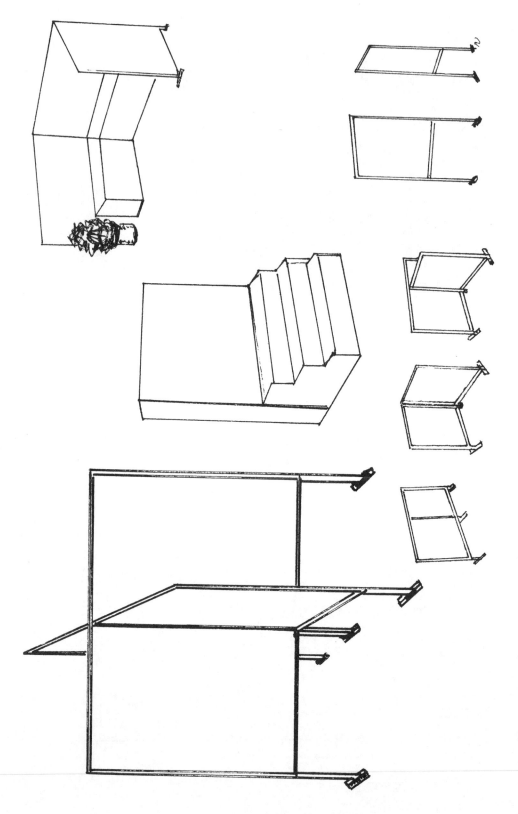

Illus. 77.   MOVABLE BULLETIN BOARDS, SCREENS

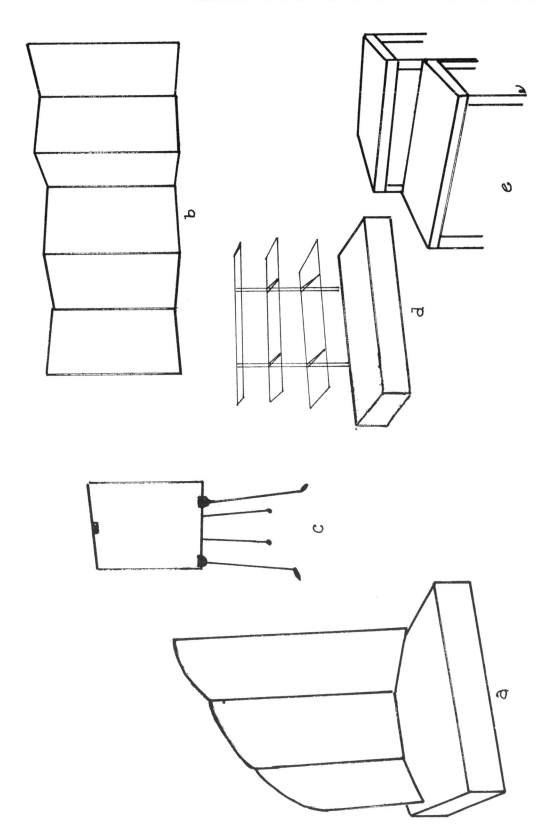

Illus. 78. DISPLAY SURFACES

Illus. 79. FIGURES TO MAKE A POINT

Illus. 80.   EVERYONE IS RAVING ABOUT ...

Illus. 81.   EXPERIENCE THE DELIGHTS OF READING, LISTENING, VIEWING

Illus. 82.   MANNEQUINS AND
LIBRARY BAG

Illus. 83.   MASKS

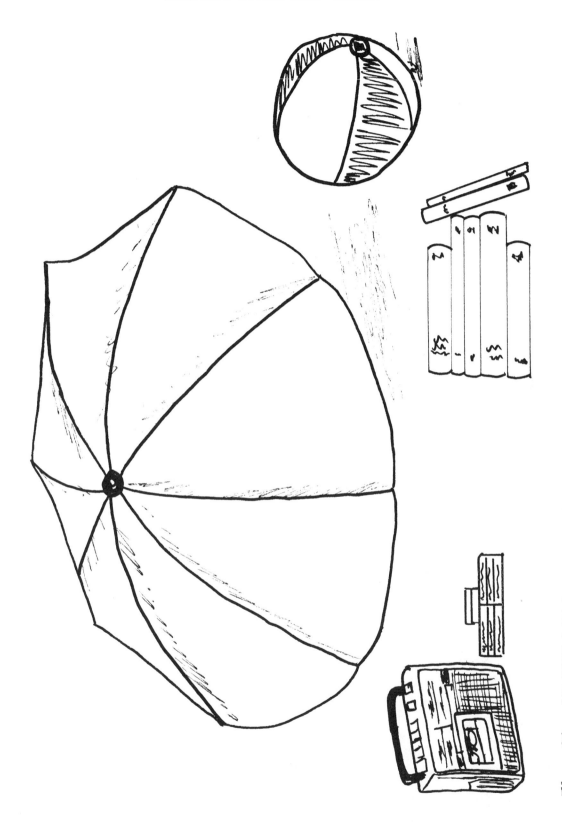

Illus. 84.   AT THE BEACH

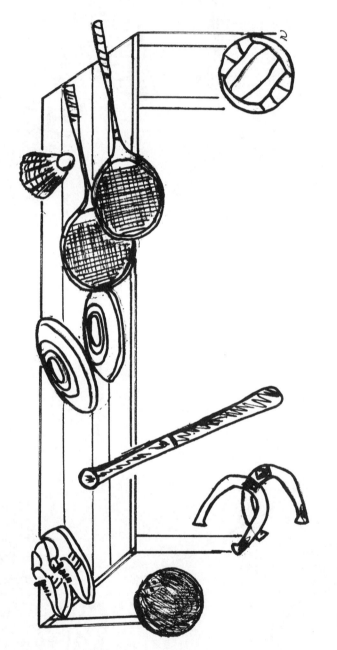

Illus. 85. SPORTS

Illus. 86.   BLACK BELT

Illus. 87.   YOU'VE GOT A WORLD OF ENTERTAINMENT

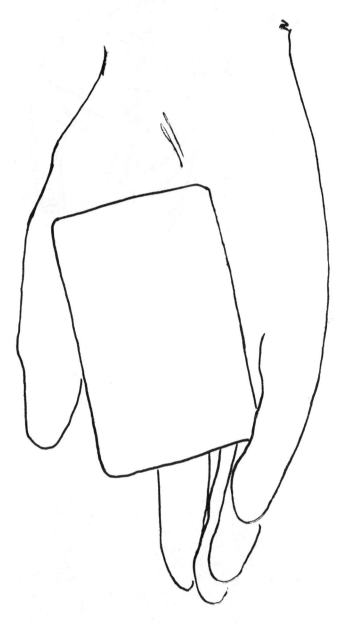

Illus. 88.   PALM

Illus. 89. HAND PATTERN

Illus. 90.   TURN BACK THE CLOCK TO 1900

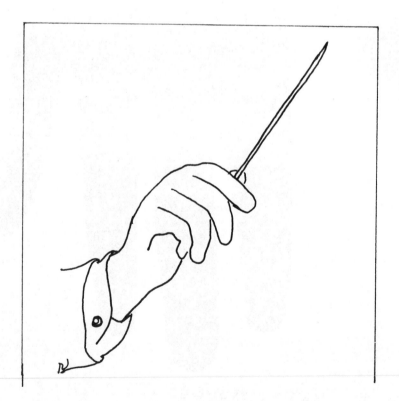

Illus. 91.   HAND WITH BATON

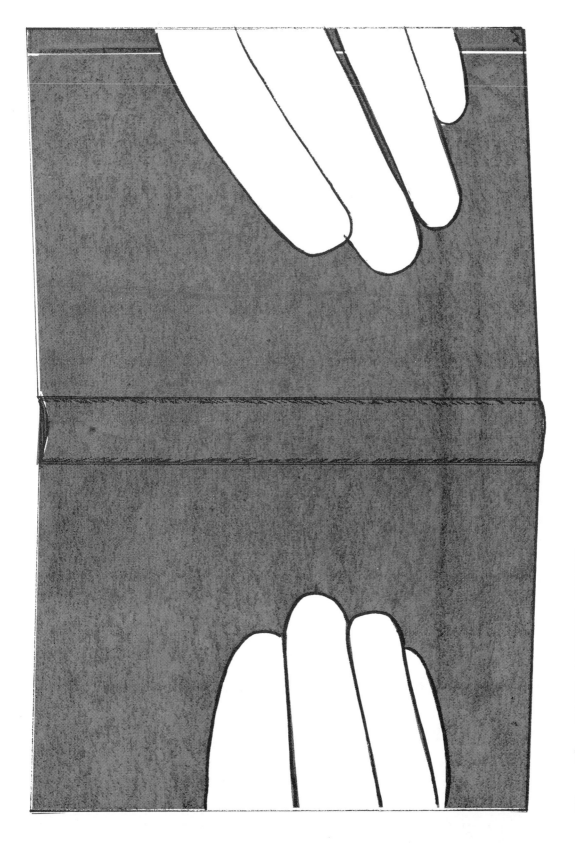

Illus. 92. HAND AROUND BOOKS

Illus. 93.   CHILDREN AND BOOKS

CAMERAS

Objective of the display:

To show how the photographer and cameraperson tell a story, whether through a single photograph or through a show of stills, slides, movies, or videotapes.

To demonstrate the role played by the developing process.

To feature the library's materials on photography, cinematography, videotaping and allied materials on light and vision.

To provide a visual history of the form that began in France in 1826, with the first known photograph by Nicéphore Niepce; that continued with the work of Louis J. M. Daguerre and Fox Talbot; that advanced through the use of chemically treated glass ("wet") plates as film in the 1860s and the development of dry plates in 1876; and that was popularized following perfection of the film roll and the Kodak camera in the 1890s.

To catch patrons in the act of using materials and facilities in the library and the staff in the act of assisting them.

To feature the work of area photographers and cameramen/camerawomen.

To introduce the wide range of photographic applications.

Adjuncts to the display:

The obvious approach is to plan a series of programs on choosing, using, and caring for cameras; on the techniques of picture-taking; and on the accessories for picture-taking. To do this, make contact with people in photo shops, with members of photography clubs, with professional photographers, and with school and college instructors of photography. Include still photography, cinematography, and videotaping. Don't neglect the

Illus. 94.　MOVIE-CAMERA SETUP

camera's role in the printing industry (including copying machines), in security systems, in science (especially astronomy and medicine), and in industry.

Along with camera basics (usually an introduction to cameras and accessories), set up clinics on specific problems in photography. These can include the correct choices of film, lighting, and framing; studio shots, action photos, and candid snapshots; choice of subject; vacation photography; photographing people; and planning slide, movie, and videotape shows.

Announce (or advertise) that the library is able to help vacationers get data on their destinations so that planning of photographic pursuits takes place prior to going.

Arrange for people with expertise in slide and movie presentations to be available at specific times to give personal assistance to people who want to learn how to develop their own shows.

Set up a "young photographers series" to help children gain experience in photography.

Switching to another area, create programs on "advertising photography" to illustrate how photographs are planned and executed; what it is like to be a photographer's model and the different kinds of photographer's models (high fashion is only one aspect); how to be ad-wise (is the "plumber" who is pictured really a plumber, and if so, does he or she really use the product advertised?).

Provide a program on innovations in the camera industry. Among the possibilities: "Home Video vs. Home Movies: A Comparison of Cost and Convenience"; "Two-Way TV: Combining Cameras and Computers for Conversation and Courses"; or "Two-Way TV: Convenience or Surveillance?"; "Videodisk Systems."

Provide a program that traces the development of ways to view photographs, including stereoscopes, viewmasters, videodisks, tachyscopes, movie projectors.

Run a series on travel with films rounded out by books, newspaper travel sections, and magazines.

Set up a demonstration on color film (with prints of the turn-of-the-century autochrome color method, those following the 1935 invention of Kodachrome color film--by Leopold Godowsky and Leopold Mannes--and modern-day improvements and variations).

Do a program on the growing trend of investing in photography (as opposed to simply being a collector without the idea of making money on resale).

Do a series on movies of past decades, trends in current filmmaking, great film directors, significant films on a particular topic (such as the development of cinematography as an art, film as social commentary, film about the Wild West).

Discussion of the display:

"Stories in Sight" features a slide show (or a series of slide shows) with a display of library materials that were used for researching it. The show can be on such subjects as travel destinations or a local event, or can be a documentary. The originator of the slide show should work up an outline that demonstrates to the viewers how the show was based on a theme and that it was built on a strong, interesting story with a beginning, middle, and end. (See Illus. 95, which can double as a screen when the center section sheet is pulled down.)

"Good, Better, Best: How to Click in Photography" is a display of photos that shows good, passable, and bad shots of the same subject, with information cards describing the conditions in each case. Illus. 96 shows a possible way to combine photos with information cards in a variety of settings.

"A Sweep of Human Vision" can be the title of a display of books of photographs with biographies of the photographers and descriptions of the cameras and techniques used. Some early names to include are André Kertész, Harry Callahan, Robert Frank, Ansel Adams, Edward Weston, Walker Evans, Henri Cartier-Bresson, Brassaï, and Alfred Stieglitz. Relative unknowns, such as Joseph Mora, come to light because they have made a significant contribution to ethnography. Mora, working with one of the first Kodak box cameras, took photographs of the Hopi Indians during the early part of the twentieth century. You will find others, equally unknown and equally significant.

For the children's section, mount a display on how to make a camera out of a cylinder. This simple instrument replicates the early camera obscura. This can be a participatory display, with the youngsters making the cameras on the spot under the guidance of an adult or a very capable young person. (See Illus. 97.)

"Flash! See All About Us!" is a display about news and feature photography in your local newspaper. It can be mounted in cooperation with the photography and local-news departments (perhaps even the librarian) of your area paper. You'll want to feature more than photographs, however. Show how the process begins with the editor's decision for the photograph to be taken and proceed to the composite sheet, which is marked to show which picture will be developed; the crop markings on enlargements; and the final printed edition. You might even want to illustrate the color-separation process for printing photographs in color in the newspaper. (See Illus. 98.) Add library materials on photojournalism.

"How We Developed" can be a historical view of the community, but it can also be a personal story of someone who was photographed from infancy into adulthood, or of a family as it grew and changed. Here, you might enjoy adding cooperation with the historical and genealogical societies to your already established association with the newspaper. Follow a specific theme, or be general, depending upon the kinds of materials available. Spark the photographs with memorabilia, clothing, artifacts, news articles, and so on. (See Illus. 99.)

"Find Your Face" is a display of photographs taken of people while in the library. Caption the photos, or simply leave it wide open for people to identify the subjects. (See Illus. 100.)

"Famous" is a display of photos of famous people, with books by and about them scattered around. An added gimmick is to have had the photographs autographed or to have sent away for "fan" pictures that come already autographed. Something like this requires planning; it can follow the same kind of time line that you used in mounting displays shown in Illus. 76 and 77. (For a possible display sketch, see Illus. 101.) Of added interest are local ties with famous people. Display photos of the mayor during a visit with the President of the United States.

"Simulation Studio" can be an audience-participation display that is set up for people to take photographs of a still life or for people to be models in photographs that are taken by a professional in the library. Obviously, there has to be the capability for many people to have the opportunity to participate. You'll want to keep track of the names and addresses of people so that each photograph can be identified and mounted to go along with the display.

The above suggestion is for still photography, but the studio situation can be recreated for videotaping, and in special circumstances you can think in terms of television and moviemaking simulations.

Another display, on a totally different track, is one that illustrates ways to view the product of the camera (film), with the range going from the stereoscope, to viewmaster, to projector, to the television in its many forms, to videodisks and whatever innovations are on deck at this point in time.

"Almost As Good As Being There: The Armchair Traveler" can feature showings of travelogs, with travel posters as backdrops, travel books and magazines, regional books, and so on. It perhaps bears saying at this point that in all of the displays, feature large-print and talking materials along with regular-print and regular-recorded materials. Illus. 102 is an idea for the display format for a bulletin board to announce events.

Another participatory display involves creating "moving cartoons." You need "an expert" who is capable of working with others, table space, and materials that include film and felt-tip pens along with paper and pencil to help people sketch ideas to be developed. You can have individuals do a segment on their own, or you can run this as a communal project with each person getting a specific number of frames to fill in. The end result can be rather interesting, depending upon the strength and flexibility of the script.

If they are available, your local movie house can help you mount a display of posters of old films that made cinema history. Along with this, you can pull out books, plays, biographies, autobiographies, historical novels, fiction, science fiction, or exposés that have been the basis for films.

"Life off Celluloid" can be a catch-all for the abundance of screen-star stories. Pin up the title and place the materials all around for browsing and borrowing. Illus. 103 is a sketch. (Use a defunct film reel as a prop or place promotional photos in facsimile film footage.)

If possible, mount a display identifying the process of filmmaking.

Cameras are made up, among other components, of convex and concave lenses. This is an extension of the human eye. Thus, a display of "Light and Vision" compares the way in which the eye sees with how the camera records. Work with specialists to mount an informative display. The same treatment applies to the concepts of "Realism and Perspective," which can combine geometry with the arts--one of which is photography. Illus. 104 is a sketch of what the camera will show as a result of the same model being photographed from different angles. You will want to have a local photographer provide enlargements of this. However, also have the model there and let people walk around the model to experience what the photographer and camera capture for us to see.

"Differences of the Same" is a puzzling headline that can combine a variety of ideas. One is to display the same model, scene, or still life as seen in a photograph, line drawing, oil painting, watercolor, and cartoon. Another idea is to show the same scene as photographed during different times of the day and during different seasons of the year. Still a third idea is to have several photographers photograph the same scene and see what happens!

Illus. 105 provides several ideas for display surfaces to hang framed photographs. If your library lacks a spare wall, utilize movable units that can be placed according to the most advantageous use of space.

Illus. 106 is a potpourri of possibilities to draw attention to thematic statements that include:

"Focus on the Subject of Your Choice"

"Focus on (name of subject)"

"Develop a Taste for Reading (Listening, Viewing ...)"

"Enlarge Your View of the World"

"Put the Library in YOUR Picture"

Sketch "a," because it is a familiar "old-type" camera, calls attention to a display of materials on historical subjects. Figure "d," a sketch of one of W. H. Fox Talbot's calotype-process cameras, piques our interest because it isn't something we see too often. It can be a good visual for a display of books on inventions.

Sketch "e" is a dramatic representation of film. Cuttings of the "real" thing can be mounted on clear paper and stretched between nylon thread to focus on a particular topic.

Make a larger-than-life prototype of the 35mm film cartridge and use it to make a point, such as "Put the Library in YOUR picture."

Sketch "c" is a stylization of a 35mm camera. Sketch "d" illustrates that you can "make" display cameras with a rectangular box for the body, a tube for the lens, and small boxes for the mechanical aspects of the camera. In place of the "real thing," several of these models can be hung or placed in strategic spots to draw attention to a point, such as "Focus on Current Fiction" for recent acquisitions or "Traveling! Put the Library in Your Picture" for light reading while you're getting there or after you've arrived.

Illus. 94, which introduced this section, draws attention to the impact of film and television on books and vice versa. It can be a dramatic window display with real lights, camera, and books perched on stools or cylinders, or it can be a silhouette of lights and camera framing a setup of books anyplace within the library.

Just as the box camera was, for a long time, the usual design in the instrument of photographers, so the box, in its variety of commercial and private uses, is a most mundane container capable of being used to create startling effects for library displays. The next section has several surprises you'll want to unwrap.

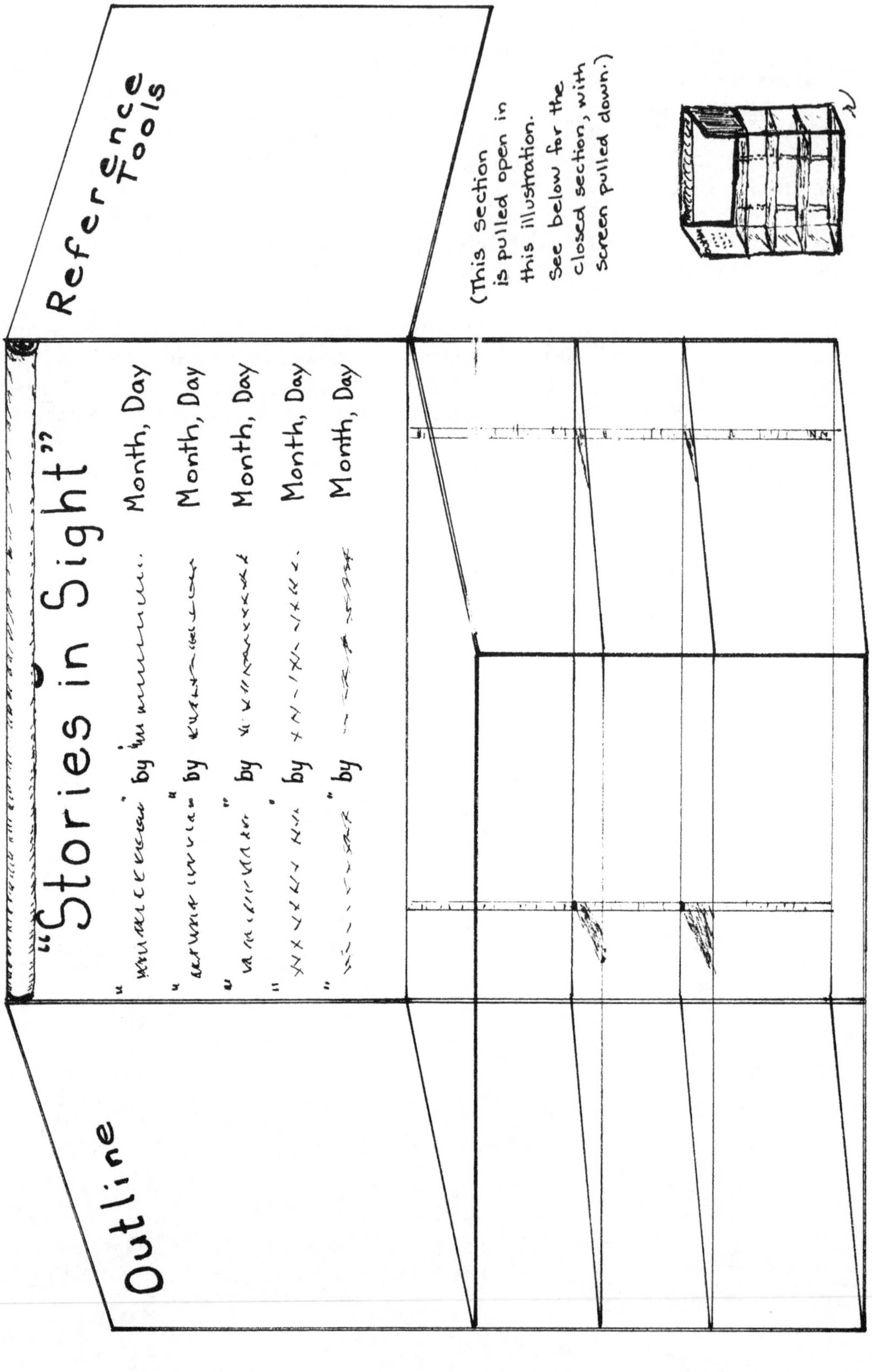

Reference
Tools

(This section
is pulled open in
this illustration.

See below for the
closed section, with
screen pulled down.)

"Stories in Sight"

"~~~~~~~~~" by ~~~~~~.... Month, Day

"~~~~~~~~" by ~~~~~~~~ Month, Day

"~~~~~~~~" by ~~~~~~~~ Month, Day

"~~~~~~~" by ~~~~~~~~ Month, Day

"~~~~~~" by ~~~~~~~~ Month, Day

Outline

Illus. 95. STORIES IN SIGHT

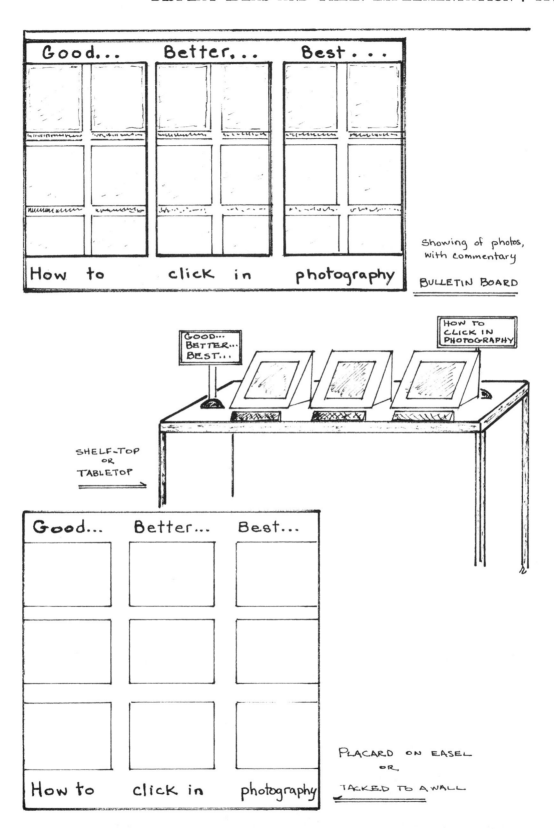

Illus. 96. GOOD, BETTER, BEST: HOW TO CLICK IN PHOTOGRAPHY

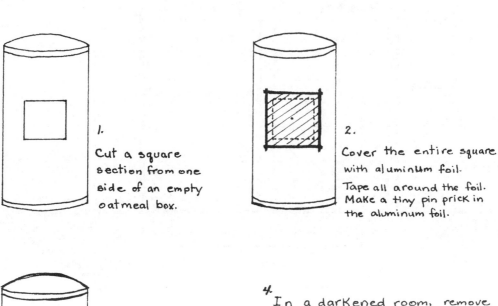

1.
Cut a square section from one side of an empty oatmeal box.

2.
Cover the entire square with aluminum foil.

Tape all around the foil. Make a tiny pin prick in the aluminum foil.

3.
Cover the foil with a flap of oil cloth that is taped only on one side.

4.
In a darkened room, remove lid from box.

Place shiny side of film toward the hole in the aluminum foil.

Tape the film to the underside of the foil.

Replace lid on box.

Be certain oil cloth covers aluminum foil.

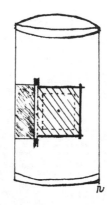

5.
Place box - oil cloth covering aluminum foil - in sunlight.
Turn in direction of object or scene to be photographed. Remove oil cloth. Leave hole in foil exposed for several seconds. Cover hole. Take box to darkened room.
Remove film to be developed.

Basic Steps For Making a Camera
From an Oatmeal Box (CAMERA OBSCURA)

Illus. 97.   MAKE YOUR OWN CAMERA

Illus. 98.   FLASH!!   SEE ALL ABOUT US!

John Jones : Pharmacist

sketch of a case display of photos and
partial memorabilia covering infancy
to adulthood.

Illus. 99.   HOW WE DEVELOPED

Illus. 100. FIND YOUR FACE

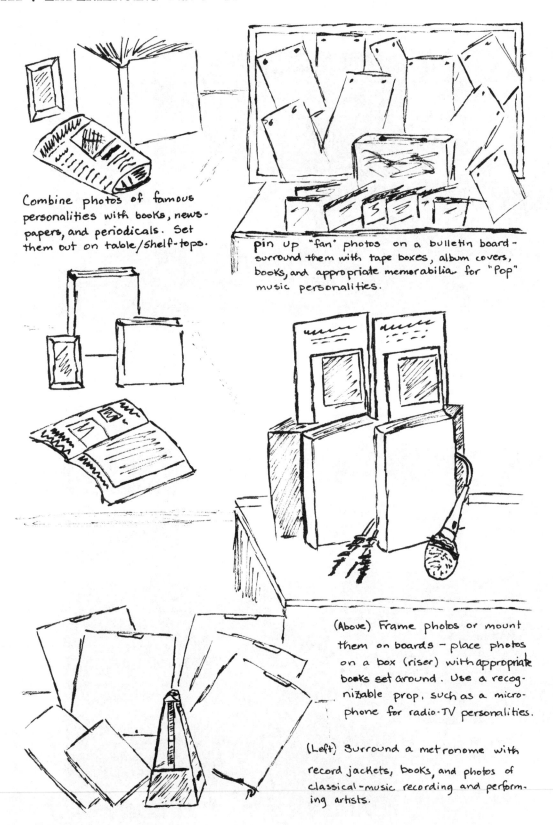

Combine photos of famous personalities with books, newspapers, and periodicals. Set them out on table/shelf-tops.

pin up "fan" photos on a bulletin board — surround them with tape boxes, album covers, books, and appropriate memorabilia for "Pop" music personalities.

(Above) Frame photos or mount them on boards — place photos on a box (riser) with appropriate books set around. Use a recognizable prop, such as a microphone for radio-TV personalities.

(Left) Surround a metronome with record jackets, books, and photos of classical-music recording and performing artists.

Illus. 101.   FAMOUS

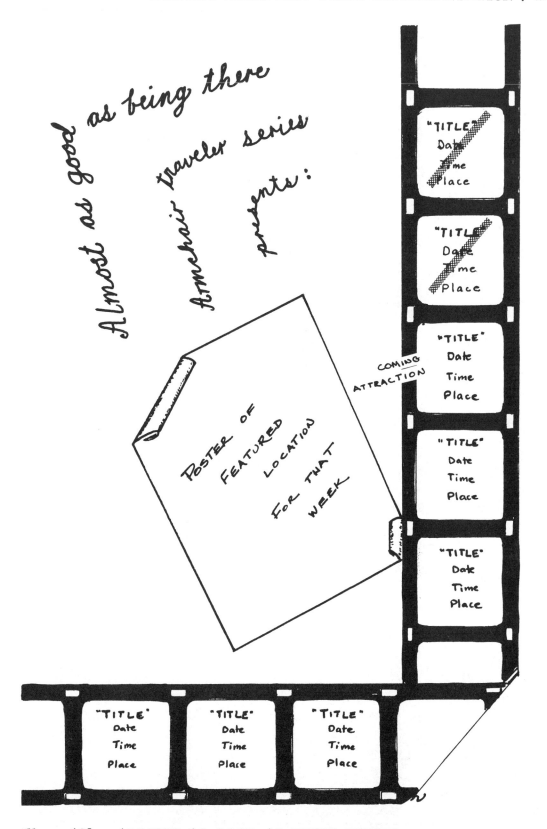

Illus. 102.   ALMOST AS GOOD AS BEING THERE

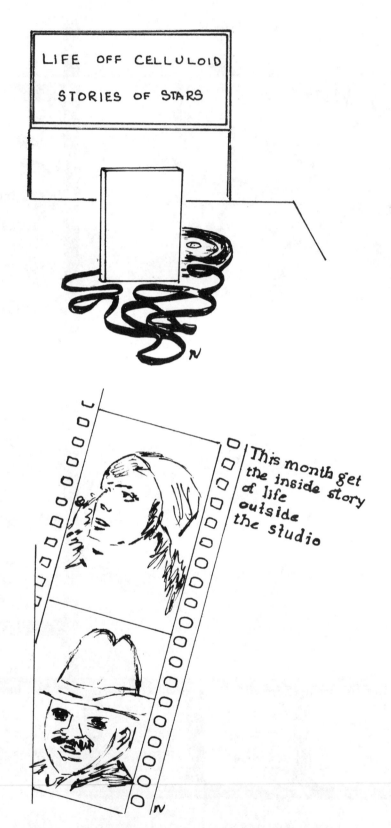

Illus. 103.   LIFE OFF CELLULOID

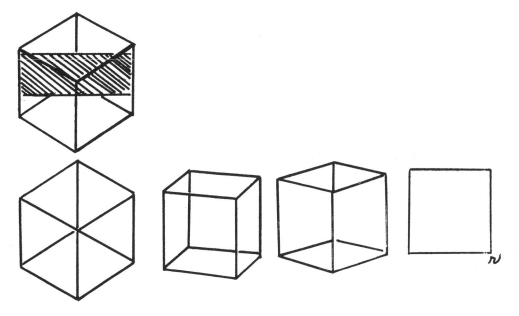

Illus. 104.   SAME SUBJECT, DIFFERENT ANGLES

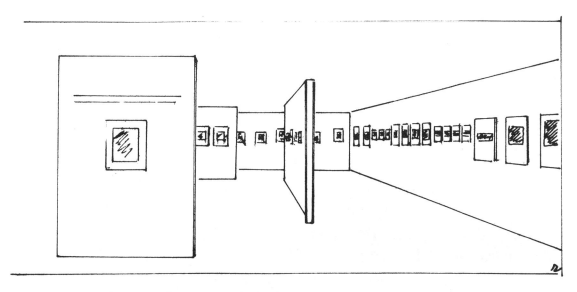

Illus. 105.   GALLERY SETUP

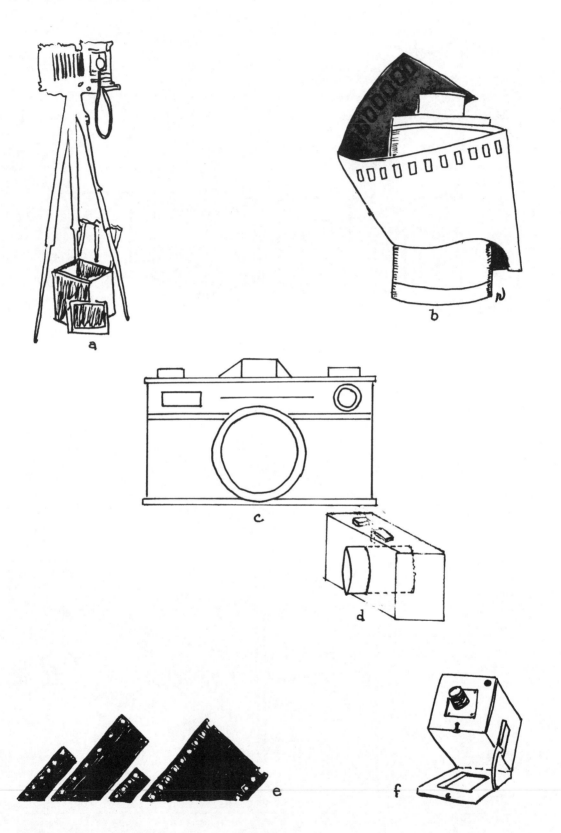

Illus. 106.   POTPOURRI OF IDEAS

IN CONCLUSION

It is time now to move from the highly visual stimuli prevalent in the preceding pages to mainly verbal suggestions so that you can let your own creative juices flow. Some displays are created when everyday objects become exciting ways to show off the library. One particular display theme started, for me, on a purely intellectual level. I looked up the word "box" to determine its origin. I got more than I bargained for.

"Box," I learned, can mean many things, depending upon context. Thus, while Gertrude Stein may have decided that "a rose, is a rose, is a rose ...," she would not have concluded that a box, is a box, is a box.

The first dictionary citation for box refers to trees, principally an evergreen or shrub mainly used for bordering flower beds. However, both the African box ("Myrsine Africana") and any of the Australian varieties ("Eucalyptus, Murraya and Tristania") are used for the manufacture of fine furniture and for scientific and musical instruments.

On further investigation, I learned of the boxberry, one variety of which is known as wintergreen and another as partridgeberry. I learned of the box elder, the boxthorn, and the boxwood.

Regarding etymology of the word, it is listed as "a box, chest" in Anglo-Saxon. The Greek pyxos means "the box tree." The Latin buxus is "anything made of boxwood"--hence, the "box" as a container. However, the precise form and use of "box" as a container can be of an infinite variety. Some may think of a wrapped gift box; some of fancy metal boxes, such as those containing special teas or delicate wafers; some of lunch boxes; some of a jack-in-the-box or a music box; some of a scented softwood cigar box; others of a box with inlaid woods polished to a satin shine; and still others, of the ingenuity of the American eggbox!

A sailor may think of the box that contains the mariner's compass, of the box chronometer, and of boxhauling as being particular to the nautical life. A carpenter's reference may be to a toolbox, a trucker's to the seat in a truck (a "box"), a banker's to a safe-deposit box, a parish priest's to

127

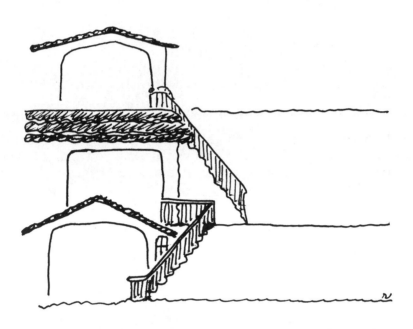

Wander where you will,
but come home to the
. . . . Public Library!
street address . . . .
city, state, zip code . . . . .
a.c., tel. no. . . . .

Hours:

Days ... Times
Days ... Times

Illus. 107.   WANDER WHERE YOU WILL,
BUT COME HOME TO THE
_____ PUBLIC LIBRARY

a contribution box. Theater managers may think of box seats, newspeople of the press box. Politicians speak of the ballot box; models carry a hatbox. Most of us use a pill box, but some chic lady may wear one.

A sportsman talks of a grouse box, of a warm box coat, or of a boxer in a boxing match. A military person may refer to a sentry box, a lawyer to a jury box, and mail carriers to a letter box. Baseball players are aware of the batter's box, the pitcher's box, and their box scores. Biologists may be concerned with boxcrabs, boxfish, box oysters, box turtles, and boxers (as related to the bulldog).

Someone from the newspaper composing room puts together a box story. Mechanics work with a journal box, box metal, box couplings, box keys, and box locks. The comma box is of importance to a printer, the box beam and box drain to an architect. Railroaders concern themselves with boxcars, interior decorators with box pleats, and furniture salespeople with box springs. Butchers know about box holly, tanners about box calf, and you, the reader of this book, will readily recall the box camera from the discussion in the previous section.

Does all of this conjure up display possibilities for your library? For me, valid objectives can be:

1) To feature the research, reference, and cataloging aspects of the library by using a vehicle of widespread interest that is indeed full of pleasant surprises.

2) To illustrate how much fun it is to wonder about a word and to pursue a private (or public) quest for information.

3) To involve a cross-section of the community as participants in a planned library activity.

Headline the statement, "Bring on the Box" and fill a case with boxes--the real objects when possible, photographs and drawings when not. Put some of them out for people to rummage through or examine, such as what makes up a household toolbox, a utility sewing box, a child's toy box, a beginner's paint box, an actor's makeup box, a building's fuse box. Use information cards to tell something pertinent about the object and to give directions on where in the library more information is available. Tag the shelves where the materials are located so they can be found easily.

Arrange a display of lunch boxes from over the years. Surround them with materials on nutrition and recipes. Invite patrons to contribute their favorite lunch-box ideas.

Involve the craft-minded with displays of workshops on origami and découpage boxes. Arrange a demonstration-display of gift-wrapping techniques. Set up a woodworking series on how to make shadow boxes. Call out collectors to bring in and tell about their filled shadow boxes.

Show off boxes as toys, puzzles, and games over the years. Feature music boxes. Demonstrate boxes as musical instruments, especially percussion and string instruments. Show the step-by-step evolution of a violin from tree to concert instrument. If a violin-maker is available to show how a violin is made, so much the better. In any case, have someone demonstrate the playing of instruments based on the box. The African box drum has been gaining popularity as a solo and ensemble instrument in elementary schools, so look for people to demonstrate this, too.

"Box," as a noun, is also "a blow, a clap," such as a box to the ear. As a transitive verb, "box" means "to strike with the hand or fist, especially on the ear." As an intransitive verb, box is defined as "to use the fists; to spar with boxing gloves; also to be a boxer." Thus, a viable display is that of the sport of boxing, including the equipment, rules and regulations, training techniques, promotion, and personalities past and present.

Think in terms of the commercial uses of boxes and arrange a display of packaging and shipping concurrent with a lecture on packaging and shipping as aspects of marketing. Feature boxes as art objects, as utility objects, as mysterious objects (the magician always uses boxes in a "magic act"). Set out craft books with designs for converting boxes of all kinds into "animals," toys, useful household containers, and expansions of the imagination. Illus. 108 shows a half-dozen possibilities. Illus. 109 is of photographs in the Normal (Illinois) Public Library. A cigar box becomes a setting for stuffed tigers and, with plants, calls attention to the 500 section in the children's room. A series of boxes become a cutaway dollhouse, decorated and furnished for family life. It is protected with a plastic sheet held on by five screws.

In addition to recreating settings from stories, use boxes as the settings from which stories are told, namely as puppet stages. Set out the books (with directions), some examples, and a collection of materials to create a participatory display. Remember to include shoebox possibilities along with the large-sized shipping boxes.

Fill boxes with specially grouped library items and offer them as "take-homes" to shut-ins of all ages. Package items specifically for weekend enjoyment for every possible clientele. Pull together materials on a specific topic and box them as a unit. Illus. 110 offers a display to catch several takers.

Put cassette-tape boxes on display with corresponding print materials. (See Illus. 111.) Don't wait for an election to draw attention to the current-events material that helps people be informed. Make your point with a display, such as the one sketched in Illus. 112. Place in it daily papers, periodicals, reports, minutes of local elected bodies, books on current issues, and written opinions of local residents.

Box off bulletin-board, wall, or end-of-shelf space. Illus. 113 offers two dramatic possibilities. In "a," the suggestion is to back the area with a nonfade material and to create boxes by outlining with a highly contrasting color of yarn or some other nonfade fabric. The idea for "b" lends itself to creating a calendar of the month. Once made, it can be used throughout the year by changing the name of the month and adjusting the number of days. Have children draw pictures for events for each day, be those events of national or local importance. Birthdays of the great and the not-so-great are always of interest. Special days should be noted, along with historic dates.

Illus. 114, 115, and 116 offer other ideas for utilizing boxes as containers, as cubes for building display space, and as alternatives for traditional storage units. In Illus. 114, "a" and "d" are self-standing box units that can be moved around as needed throughout the library. Their contents can be varied as the need arises. Sketch "b" suggests a way to make the shelving of odd-sized boxes easier in the toddlers' section. Merely box the titles of a specific genre and put them on a floor-level shelf for easy use. Sketch "c" is an idea for a movable display box with bands for holding such materials as books, recordings, and periodicals. It, too, is portable, as is "e," which is a box of many uses, open and closed, with a carrying handle. Sketches "f" and "h" are variations on the old telephone-booth concept. They create intimate display areas. Sketch "g" is a nostalgic throwback to the wooden orange crate. As a unit, it can be moved and set up with any number of other props, such as plants, screens, or mannequins.

Sketch "a" in Illus. 115 suggests combining screens with cubes for a variety of display surfaces. Figure "b" is a possibility for an information center; "c" is an overgrown box kite with poster space available on the four sides of the top and bottom units and the open middle section serving as a good place to put something touchable on view. Illus. 116 combines cubes of various heights for a display surface, in this case of reference materials.

There are hundreds of other items that lend themselves to use as props or as themes to feature any library's materials, services, and programs. Events in the community also prompt display possibilities. A word, a group of words, a slogan used to sell a product or a piece of clip art can be transformed into a library display. A random selection follows:

THE SPICE RACK--"Put Spice in Your Life"

Label facsimiles of spice bottles with topics from adventure to zen. Make this an opportunity to describe spices and their value in everyday life, from adding aroma to providing zest in the foods we eat. Use materials and programs in the library as a parallel.

BUILDINGS--"A Library Book Is Excellent for Every Decor"

Feature models and blueprints with books around them. Topics can include alternative energy sources and the architectural and decorating philosophy behind them. There is a growing list of novels that have houses or buildings in general as a major factor in the weaving of the story.

Place door and window frames around sections of the library to feature them or simulate a window, as in Illus. 117, to lend a special mood.

For the young-adult section, place a half-pulled-down (or pulled-up) shade on a window frame. Place the headline "HELLO WORLD" on the shade. On the other side of the window frame, feature books that cover any number of topics. Next to a model of a skyscraper, add the legend, "THE HEIGHT OF EXCELLENCE IS IN YOUR LIBRARY."

FURNITURE--"Choose a Style to Enhance Your Personality"

Place materials of wide interest on top of charming étagères, painted park benches, overstuffed swivel rockers, kitchen stools, office chairs, etc.

HATS--"Hang Your Hat at the Info Place"

Place hats around the library to draw attention to the items they represent --e.g., baseball cap, fishing hat, gardening hat, golfing hat, safety helmet.

POTS, PANS, BASKETS--"Hungry for Facts? Book with Us"; "We Satisfy All Listening, Reading, Viewing Appetites"; "Recipe for Low Calorie Repast --Carrot/Celery Jumble and a Book"; "Come See What's Cooking at the Library"

Suspend items from the ceiling or place them around in unique and ordinary ways with library materials.

HOROSCOPES--"The Library Fits into YOUR Sign"

Pop the twelve signs of the zodiac all over the library in all of their various formats, from bookmarks to T-shirts. Supply information about astrology. (Some people who have a lighthearted attitude toward it may gain a bit more respect; people who are really into astrology may become less defensive.)

ALMANACS AND MOON SIGNS--"Anytime Is the Right Time at the Library"

Material on the phases of the moon, almanac covers, explanations of the force of gravity, and examples of lunar calendars help broaden interests.

DOLLAR SIGNS--"Where Else Can You Get This Much for a $[fill in the average library tax per household or per individual] Investment?"

List the actual cost of items in separate sections of the library.

With their consent, monitor the borrowings of a family or an individual over a specified period of time and itemize how much money that family or individual is saving as a result of using the library's resources.

"You Have to Spend a Little to Save a Lot ..."

The Library, It's Worth the Time and Money"

"Keep Costs Under Control ... Use the Library"

"All You Can Read, View, and Listen to for $_____ a year ... at the Library"

"There's Always Something Special at the Library"

"Borrow from Us ... and $AVE!"

      (See Illus. 118.)

STUFFED ANIMALS--"Cuddle Up with a Good Book?

Place fetching stuffed animals all over, with a book tucked alongside.

MINI-BILLBOARDS--"Take a Stand Against Boredom. Direct Your Attention to: _____"

Have a visual of a variety of exciting, entertaining, engrossing topics.

WORDS WITH A MESSAGE--"Unique"; "Indispensable"; "Subtle"; "Irresistible"; "Satisfying"; "Brilliant"; "Beguiling"

Place words, in attractive calligraphy, where they will draw attention to library materials and entice patrons to browse and borrow.

CATCH PHRASES--Typical advertising fare can be effective in a library because it is unexpected. Such phrases are also eye-catching as displays out of the library in theater lobbies, bowling alleys, laundromats, or banks. For displays out of the library, always list the name, address, telephone number, and hours open of the library.

Value Packed	Outstanding Value
Your Choice	Great Choice
New Improved	As Seen on TV!
Featured	Try the Library for a Change

Marvels Only the Most Gifted Writers Can Achieve

The Tradition

Because of Its Enduring Quality and Classic Excellence, You'll Want to Savor this Work by _____

Symbol of Leadership, Symbol of Security: Your Library Card [See Illus. 119 and 120].

March into the Library Today for Spectacular Savings [Have items "red-tagged" for people when they get there.]

$25 Book, Absolutely Free for 21 Days to Anyone with a Library Card

$100 Shopping Spree: 2 Books, 2 Records, 1 8mm Film, 1 Framed Art Reproduction: Yours for 21 Days at No Service Charge

Bargains Are Blooming at the _____ Public Library

Special Selection of Popular Fiction

All-Purpose Household Manuals

All-Weather Biographies

One of a Kind _____ [list the single titles]

Selected Titles for Men, Women, and Children

Great Listening by _____ and _____ [name groups or single performers]

Pickins-a-Plenty at the _____ Public Library

Red Tag Special Days at the _____ Public Library

There's More to Us Than Meets the Eye [headline above records and tapes]

Your Whole Family Will Enjoy _____ [list general family-interest items]

Year After Year the Library Is the Place You Can Depend On

Have a Question? We're the Answer. The _____ Public Library

Examine, at No Risk [headline with a pile of materials]

Attention Teens: Full Line of Latest Disks and Tapes ... at the _____ Public Library

Don't Miss an Author to Remember

Clearance! Entire Shelf of Gothics. Three to a Patron While Supply Lasts. 21 Days of Enjoyment Guaranteed or New Titles Cheerfully Refunded

Just What You're Looking For. Stock Up Now for Holiday Enjoyment [headline alongside cart full of selected titles that are constantly replenished]

Early-Bird Opportunities. New Titles to the First 50 Patrons.

Mother's Special Day [headline with books of special interest to mothers of all ages; do the same for all sorts of other special days]

We're Convenient ... and We're Different ... We Satisfy Your Needs at No Cost Beyond What Everyone Pays at Taxtime

We're the Money-Stretchers. Enjoy the Savings When You Borrow at the _____ Public Library

Complete from A to Z [list card-catalog entries, one per letter] at the _____ Public Library. Check Us Out.

Take the Library challenge. It'll Pay Off

Get in the Act. Hurry Down to Your Public Library and Check Out the Collection. You'll be a Winner

WANTED! Men, Women, and Children Who Like to Read. Apply at the _____ Public Library

Look at the Pluses When You Turn 60. Join the Library's Senior Club

It's the Greatest. What Is? Reading Is.

Don't Miss This Special Library Offer! [list a high-interest program at no cost to participants]

[See Illus. 120 and 121.]

Short on Cash? In Need of Entertainment? Try the _____ Public Library

Make the _____ Public Library a Regular Part of Your Schedule for:
    - Daily money-saving specials of your choice
    - Big selection--over _____ items from which to choose
    - Community (neighborhood)-owned and operated
    - Friendly service by people eager to serve you

A Touch of Class, a Spark of Warmth. The _____ Public Library for the Best Reads in Town

Discover the Outdoor Life at the _____ Public Library

Cool Graphics for Summer at the _____ Public Library

Give three cheers for _____ [list names of winning authors, composers, performing groups, teams, etc.]

They're Available at the _____ Public Library

All the Comforts of Home, None of the Distractions. The _____ Public Library Study Room

Keep Up with the World at the _____ Public Library

When Only the Best Will Do: Bring Your House Guests to the _____ Public Library

Something Different. The _____ Public Library

Consider the Novel at the _____ Public Library

A WONDERFUL IDEA: The _____ Public Library

Anything from Romance to Business in One Convenient Location: The _____ Public Library

You'll Love this 198- Version of a Favorite Standby: THE ALMANAC [or any other annual edition]. Look for It at the _____ Public Library

Gourmet Cuisine or Plain Good Cookin': Recipes from the _____ Public Library Satisfy

The Poetry Experience Is Yours at the _____ Public Library

End Information Hang-Ups. Avoid Conversation Lags. Use the _____ Public Library

Need the Right Information at the Right Time? You'll Find It at the _____ Public Library

Need a Lift? Try HUMOR at the _____ Public Library

An Impressive Choice. Found at the _____ Public Library

First-Class Travelers: Paperbacks from the _____ Public Library

A Book to Share with a Child. Get Yours at the _____ Public Library

Suggestions on Weight Maintenance. Easily Available at the _____ Public Library

The Dynamic Duo: Picture Books and Recordings. Check Them Out at the _____ Public Library

A Hostess's Best Friend [set out materials on entertaining in all sorts of situations]

Not for Experts Only [surround this announcement with practical guides for the novice in anything]

Fashion Update [put out the journals, pattern books, and newspaper columns]

Take a Frog [or any other animal] to Lunch [a perfect tag for books about an animal]

A Bit of Tropical Splendor [or of any other location--great for travel items]

Need a Better Mousetrap? Invent One [pull out the materials on inventions, patents, etc.]

No More Struggling with Tiny Type [parade out the large-print items]

Try a Little Playfulness [set out mind-stretching themes like And Rain Makes Applesauce]

For Lazin' Around [string up a hammock--small-size--and fill it with "easy reads"]

Perk Up Your Conversation [talked-about books, magazine articles, etc.]

Serenity and Understatement [poetry, pieces of sculpture]

For Connoisseurs [beautifully written books, masterful recordings]

For People Who Pursue Excitement [line up the adventure and thriller types]

Another Point of View [materials on divergent opinions]

SMALL, PERMANENT DISPLAYS--Set them up in cooperation with civic groups.

At the location of the regular monthly meetingplace for the local business association or chamber (association) of commerce, put out your latest acquisitions of interest to members. Use the running head "YOUR BUSINESS IS OUR BUSINESS." Arrange to have the books available for borrowing on the spot.
    For the photography club, bring in a display with the running head "CLICK WITH THE LATEST."
    At the local sports center, use the running head "SPORTS SPECIALS."
    The point is to bring a specialized part of the collection to a significant population of people who may not regularly use the library because it isn't convenient or because it didn't seem of personal value until it was specifically pointed out to them that the library has a lot to offer.

SPECIAL COMMUNITY DAYS--Set up displays that match the theme of the event.

If your community has a big spring event with flowers, beautification tips, etc., join in with a headline that says: "LET YOUR MIND BLOOM!" Set out rows of pots and fill them with general-interest materials that can be circulated on the spot.
    If it's a fall event, pull out bushel baskets full of wares and run a banner that announces: "HARVEST OF VALUES!"
    If the big event is a carnival or a fair or sidewalk days, change the

title and the props accordingly. If you can't spare a person to be on hand, recruit a volunteer who has a good, basic knowledge about the library and who is good at interacting with people. A silent display is better than nothing, but a display with a person available is far better all the way around in such a situation. Having the person dress according to the theme lends even more "oomph" to the project.

Don't pass up a chance to be part of a walking display, either. The library can fit into any homecoming, holiday, or parade theme. It takes some gumption, some recruiting of aid, and a good-sized sense of humor, but it can be done. It is also possible to have an annual event with the library always being represented in a specific way, such as a contingent of walking storybook characters. Familiarity need not become boredom. A tradition of clever paper-bag masks worn by people clad in black turtleneck sweaters and jeans can be effective. (See Illus. 122.) For both durability and effect coat the paper with clear plastic.

Floats are superb display opportunities. Designing and building them takes a great deal of time and requires special expertise. Some specific points to consider are:

1) Is the vehicle upon which the float is to be built sturdy and mechanically reliable?

2) Is the design of the float within the guidelines of the parade rules?

3) Does the design of the float meet the objectives of the library in entering a float?

4) Are the materials and the design right for the time of year, weather, and route conditions?

5) What are the apparent and possible hidden costs? What is the budget source?

6) What liability protection must be considered?

7) What personnel is available to oversee the production, parade, and followup procedures?

8) What immediate benefits are to be expected by the library's participation in a float entry?

9) What long-term benefits are to be expected by the library's participation in a float entry?

10) Is there an alternative way to participate and still accrue most of the above two sets of benefits?

ANNUAL REPORTS--These have gotten coverage in preceeding sections, but there may also be a need to convey special reports. Illus. 123, 124, and 125 are examples of three possible situations. Editorial comment is another way of passing on library messages. These can be tucked into a corner of displays on a regular basis, à la Ed Emberley. Done with taste and humor, these "messages" can become an appreciated and anticipated addition. Illus. 126 shows sketches of several approaches. The "vehicle" can be created from origami folding, felt, or any combination of fabrics and materials and can thus easily be moved and fit into a variety of situations. However, establish a location, such as a corner where the rabbit or the bird or the owl or the flower or the conversation balloon will always appear. Sometimes, there may not be a significant library comment, so merely have the critter or the space say, "HI!" or "Lovely display, isn't it?" or "Have you smiled at three people?"

There's an old vaudeville saying that reminds us, "Always leave them laughing when you say good-bye." So, arrange to have the exit display say something that will make people feel as though you really care that they are there, which will make them feel good. Illus. 127 provides patrons with an opportunity to say how they feel about their library experience and to come back to note what the librarians say in reply. Illus. 128 simply says thank you for coming.

The major intent of this work has been to help you generate your own creative capabilities so that you can maintain a continuous calendar of displays in your library. Three appendixes bring the book to a close. Appendix A addresses the basics of library-display philosophy and techniques through a brief outline. Display terminology is covered in Appendix B. Appendix C is a sharing of another kind. Here are photographs of displays that were up when I happened to be in a library with my camera at hand.

Taken as a whole, this book provides a beginning. Therein lies a truth: creative work is never-ending. Enjoy!

There was an old man who lived in a box. He had no shoes and two pairs of socks. He had four doors without any locks. Alas, the old man who lived in a box!

BOX MASK: FOUR FACES.

"The first little piggie built his house of straws. They were beautiful yellow straws. Then came the wolf."

"Let me in," said the wolf.

Illus. 108.   BOXES BECOME ANYTHING

Illus. 109.   BOXES TO LIVE IN

Illus. 110.   BOXES TO GO

Illus. 111.   BOXES OF CASSETTE TAPES ON DISPLAY

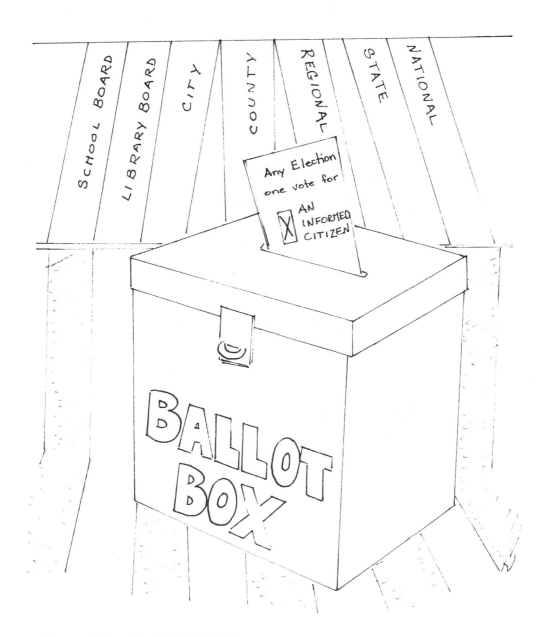

Illus. 112. BALLOT BOX

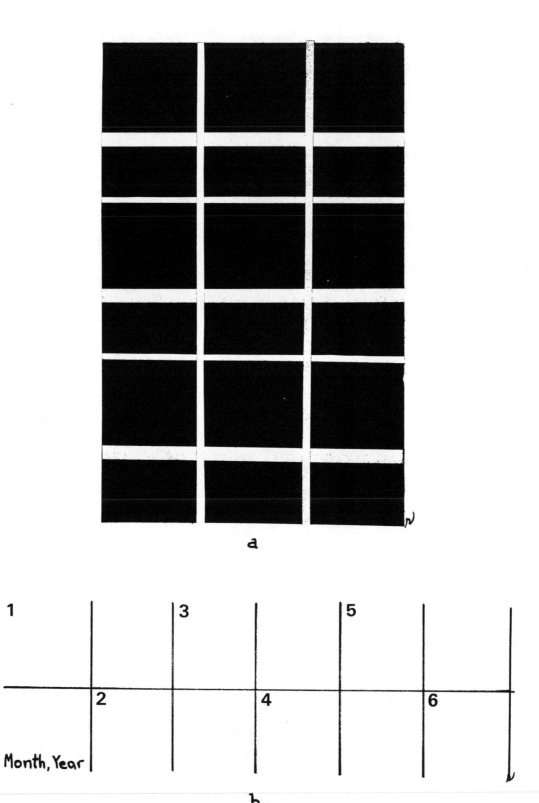

Illus. 113. "BOX OFF" A BULLETIN BOARD

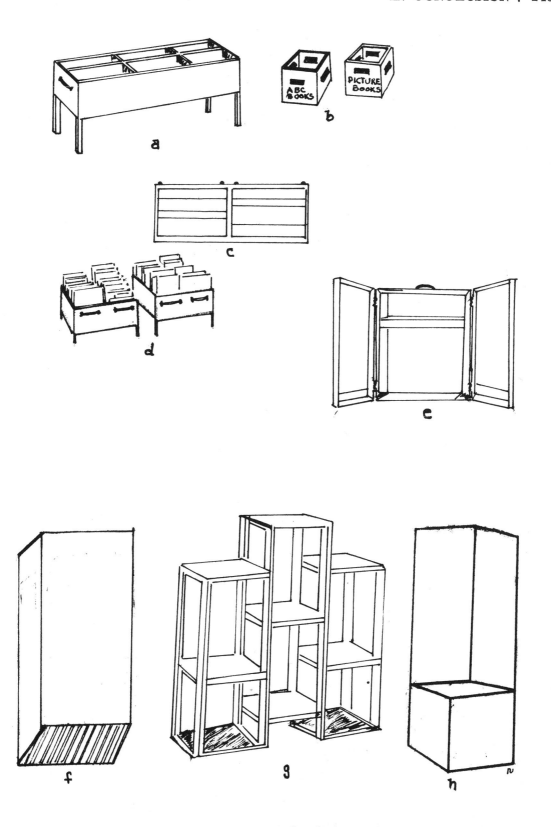

Illus. 114.   BOXES TO HOLD MATERIALS

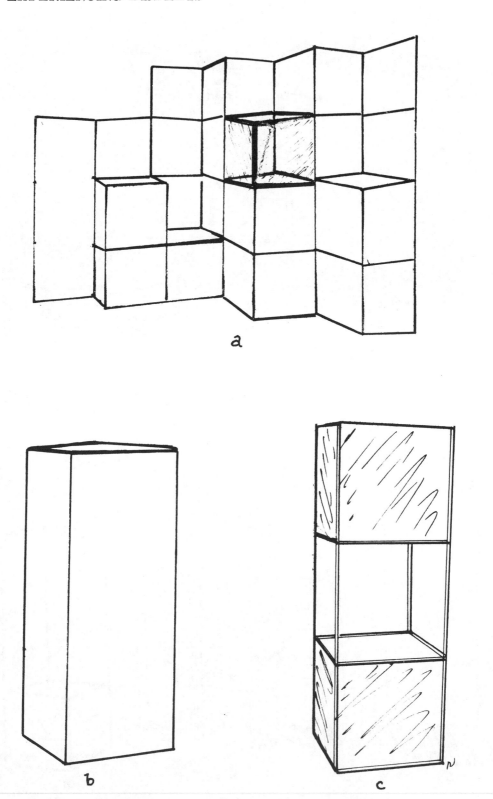

Illus. 115.   BOXES FOR DISPLAY SURFACES

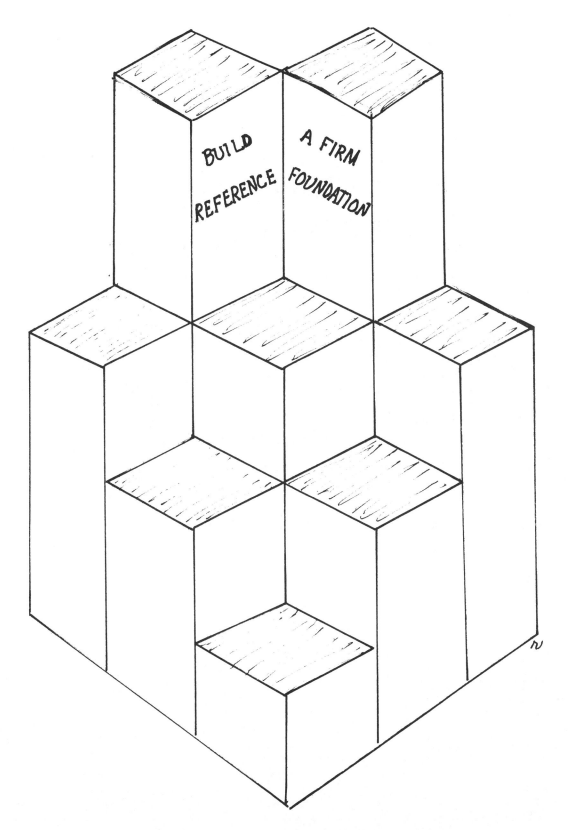

Illus. 116.   BUILD A FIRM REFERENCE FOUNDATION

Illus. 117.   WINDOW FACADE DISPLAY

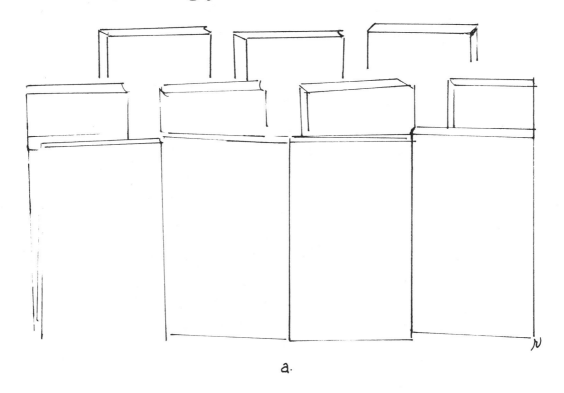

a.

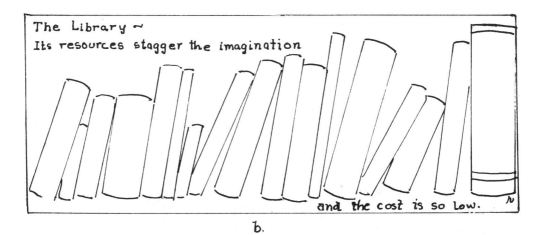

b.

Illus. 118 (a)   WHERE ELSE CAN YOU GET THIS MUCH FOR
                 $28 A YEAR?

         (b)   THE LIBRARY--ITS RESOURCES STAGGER THE
                 IMAGINATION, AND THE COST IS SO LOW

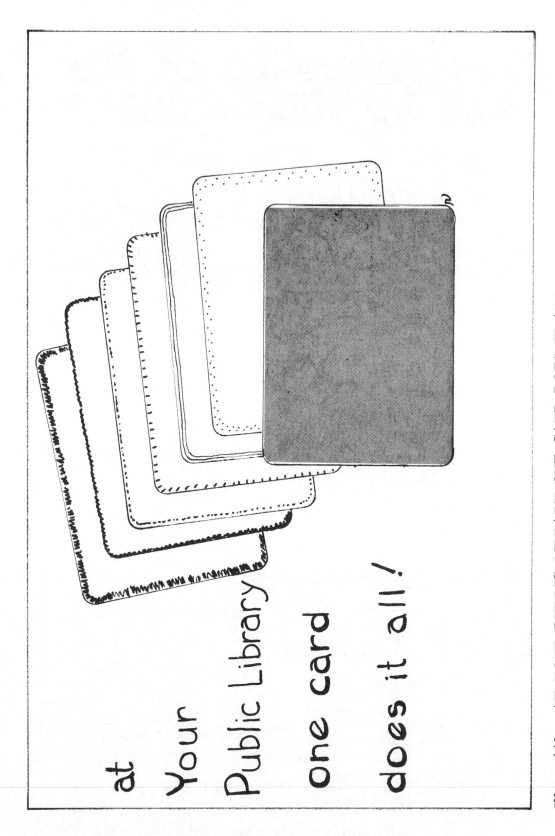

at Your Public Library one card does it all!

Illus. 119. AT YOUR PUBLIC LIBRARY ONE CARD DOES IT ALL

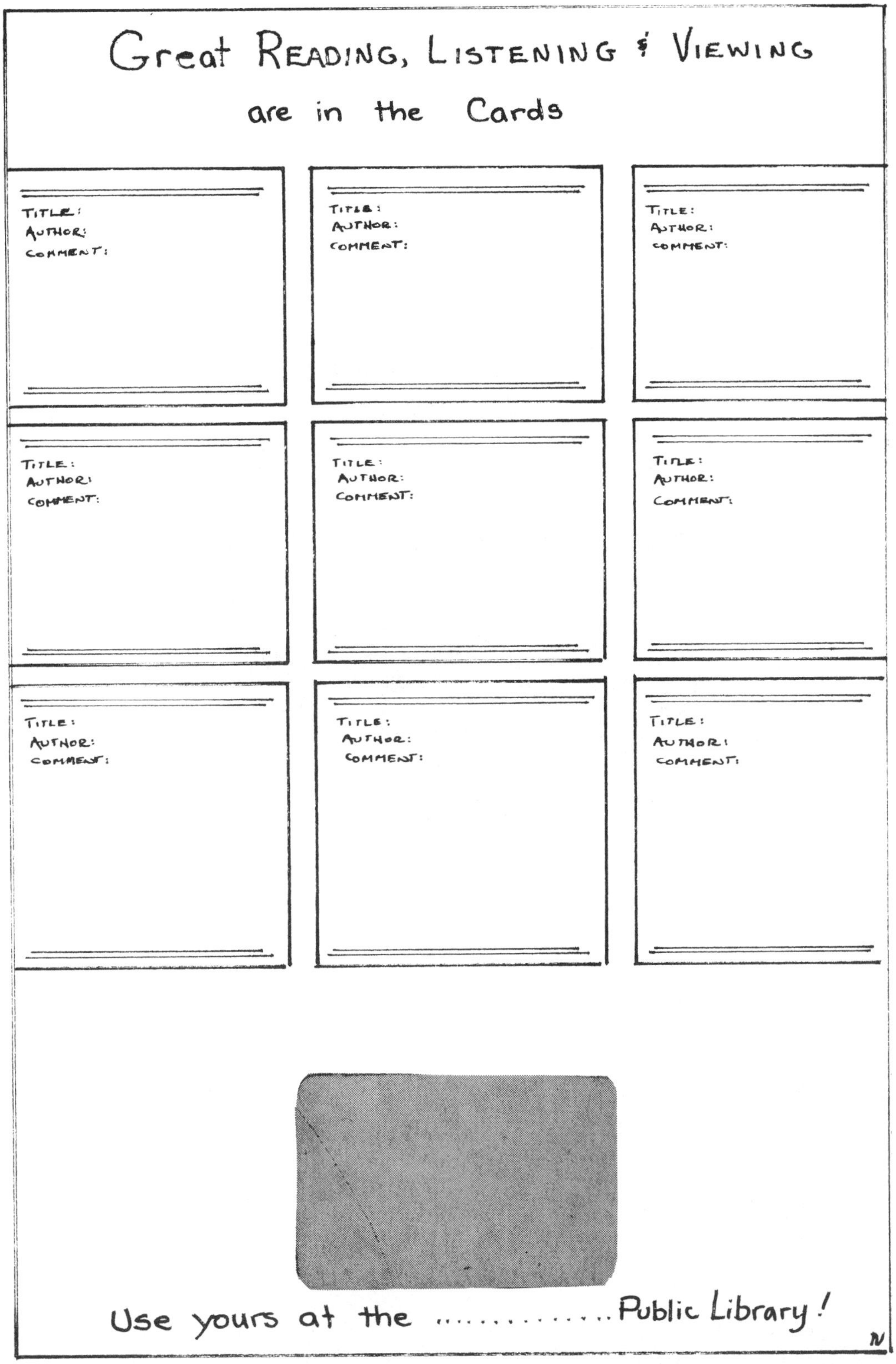

Illus. 120. GREAT READING, LISTENING, AND VIEWING ARE IN THE CARDS ... USE YOURS AT THE _____ PUBLIC LIBRARY

Discover the world
on
------------------ Street
at
------------------ Public Library

Illus. 121. DISCOVER THE WORLD

Illus. 122. PAPER-BAG MASKS

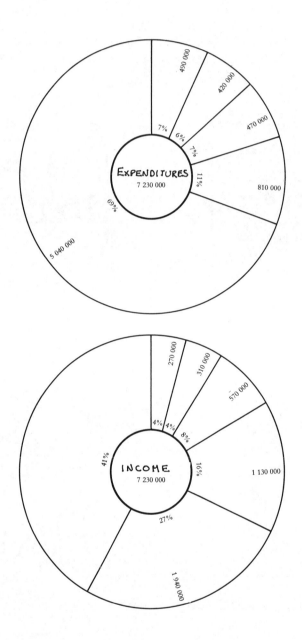

The PLAN for fiscal year 1983-84

Illus. 123.   PIE GRAPHS: THE
PLAN FOR FISCAL
YEAR 1983-84

Going...

Going...

Gone...

Inflation gobbled up our budget.
To stretch the crumbs over the next 3 months
library hours will be curtailed.

Illus. 124.   GOING ... GOING ... GONE

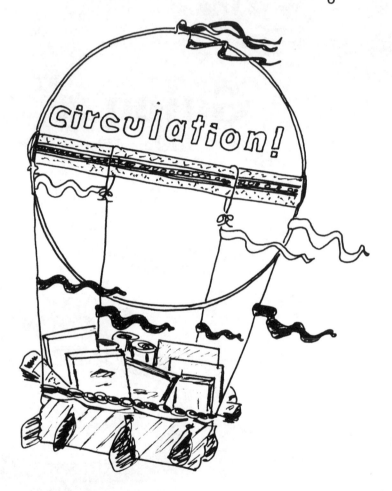

What's up at
The Library?

Circulation!

HERE ARE THE FACTS & FIGURES OF THIS
OUTSTANDING PHENOMENON :

Illus. 125.   WHAT'S UP AT THE LIBRARY?

Illus. 126.   MESSAGE MAKERS

We aim to please.
Tell us if we're on target.∗

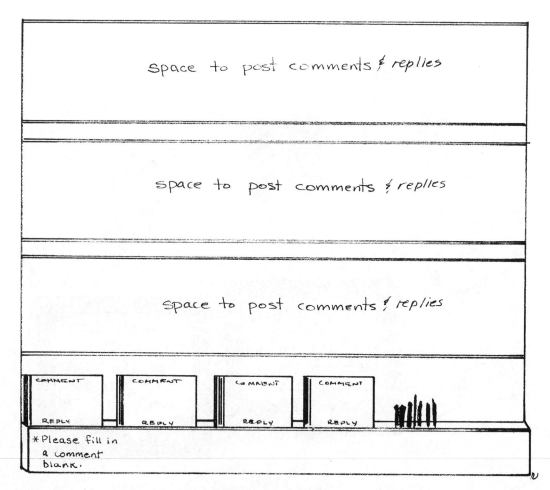

Illus. 127.   WE AIM TO PLEASE ...

Illus. 128.   THANK YOU FOR COMING

Appendix A
LIBRARY DISPLAY: PHILOSOPHY AND TECHNIQUE

Displays help library patrons "see what is available." A visual tool, display works with three other aspects of promotion--advertising, publicity, and personal selling--to reach the widest possible audience. (See You Can Do It, by Rita Kohn and Krysta Tepper [Metuchen, N.J.: Scarecrow, 1981]. Part VII, "Displays, Exhibits and Bulletin Boards" [pp. 64-76] offers guidelines and policies regarding displays in libraries.)

PROMOTION

Activities by a seller to promote
communication with potential buyers

ADVERTISING:
Paid messages in
form of:
catalogs,
direct mail,
newspapers,
radio,
television

DISPLAY:
Visual show
of merchandise

PUBLICITY:
Nonpaid media
messages about
an institution
or a product

PERSONAL SELLING:
Face-to-face contact
with a customer

Display by itself will not do the complete marketing job for the library. The four components need to be coordinated as a unit. Librarians should utilize the library's advertising budget and any free media time and space available to tell people in the community about the library's materials, services, and programs. They should also develop the potential of the library staff as topnotch salespersons through person-to-person contact and through visual presentations to groups.

Along with "selling" the library's materials, services, and programs, the four components of promotion help establish the library's image. In planning promotional activities, librarians must consider the long-range effect and make some specific decisions, including:

1) How do the library board and library staff want the library to appear in the community?

2) What community attitude toward the library do the library board and staff desire?

3) What effect should promotional activities have for the library?

4) How will the library's promotional activities be supported and managed?

While the library board establishes the public-relations philosophy, the library administrator sets the policies, including provision of the ingredients to mount displays. Four essential parts are:

1) Budget: specifically for trained personnel and for display materials and tools;

2) Personnel: individuals trained in display planning and building techniques;

3) Space: to mount displays for general viewing and for storage of display materials and tools;

4) Time: to plan, build, and dismantle displays; to coordinate displays as one component of the overall promotion package; to advertise and publicize displays to bring people in to the library to view them.

In the process of implementing display as one part of the library's promotional activities, the display specialist needs to consider two basic categories of questions (see pages 164-173 for worksheets):

GENERAL

1) How does the mounting of displays correlate with the entire library program?

2) What display locations are available?

3) What calendar of display topics is most effective in relation with the overall promotion program?

4) What kind of assistance is available in planning, mounting, and publicizing displays?

5) What kind of space is available to store materials and to build displays?

6) What materials and tools are already available for use in mounting displays?

7) How can the available budget be used to best advantage?

SPECIFIC

1) What are the objectives for this display? What messages should the viewers be getting?

2) What designs are best for the library's materials for this display?

3) What display props and fixtures are needed for this design?

4) What time elements are best for this display: planning time; building time; tenure of display to be on view; dismantling time?

5) What resources are available for assistance for this display?

6) What expenses will be incurred in planning, mounting, running, dismantling, and storing this display?

7) How should the success of the display be evaluated (staff evaluation; visitor reaction)?

Displays are not something that go up as an afterthought. They are important to the promotion, but they are equally valuable to the programming. Thus, planning is essential. The following pages are aids to help the display specialist work with the rest of the library staff for the greatest effect.

_____ LIBRARY

CORRELATION OF DISPLAYS WITH THE

LIBRARY PROGRAM: 19__

Department	Activities & materials of display capability*	Dates for display to be seen	Contact person

*1) Items that are of a "natural" interest because of:
    a) the season
    b) community events being scheduled
    c) national or international events of widespread interest
    d) economic, political, social conditions of consequence.
 2) Items that aren't currently "moving" but that would if they got some special attention, as in a display coupled with specific programming.

_____LIBRARY

INVENTORY OF DISPLAY LOCATIONS: 19__

Place	Dimensions	Possible assets	Possible liabilities
OBVIOUS LOCATIONS:			
NOT-SO-OBVIOUS LOCATIONS:			
ABSOLUTELY UNBELIEVABLE LOCATIONS:			

165

_____ LIBRARY

CALENDAR OF DISPLAY TOPICS: 19__

Date	Locations	Display theme	Library contact

_____ LIBRARY

INVENTORY OF ASSISTANCE FOR DISPLAYS: 19__

Name	Tel. no.	Kind of assistance available	Dates

_____LIBRARY

INVENTORY OF WORK SPACE: 19__

Location	Size	Advantages	Disadvantages	Dates available

_____ LIBRARY

INVENTORY OF STORAGE SPACE: 19__

Location	Size	Advantages	Disadvantages	Dates available

_____LIBRARY

INVENTORY OF AVAILABLE DISPLAY

MATERIALS & TOOLS: 19__

Item	Location	Condition it is in	Dates available

_____LIBRARY

DISPLAY BUDGET: 19__

INCOME

Source   Amount per item   Total

EXPENDITURES

Item   Cost   Total

171

_____LIBRARY

INDIVIDUAL DISPLAY PLANNING SHEET: Date _____

Theme of the display: _____
_____

Objectives of the display:

1. _____
2. _____
3. _____
4. _____

Ways in which the display correlates with the library program/Department:

1. _____
2. _____
3. _____
4. _____
5. _____
6. _____

Locations of the display and library materials to be included:

Location	Display components Library materials	Props	Surfaces	Where to get each item

Display Planning Sheet (cont.)

Sketches of display designs:

Evaluation procedure:

Contents of staff evaluation   Contents of visitor-reaction cards

Timeline: Job completed:

Coordinating _____   _____

Planning _____   _____

Publicizing _____   _____

Building _____   _____

On display _____   _____

Dismantling _____   _____

Storing _____   _____

Personnel:

Name	Job	Date to do it	Time it takes

Display Planning Sheet (cont.)

Budget:

Item	Purchased from	Cost	Total

Evaluation of the job:

Unforeseen problems: _____

_____

_____

Unforeseen bonuses: _____

_____

_____

Tips for next time: _____

_____

_____

Ideas worth pursuing: _____

_____

_____

Appendix B
TOPICAL GLOSSARY OF (LIBRARY) DISPLAY TERMINOLOGY

DISPLAY DESIGN: A plan that motivates patrons to make use of library
materials, services, and programs and that creates a favorable image
of the library in the public's mind. Specific design elements are used
to establish mood, to evoke feelings and to produce a desired reaction.

Elements of Display Design: those parts that, together, influence the
viewer's reaction.

1) Color (Hue): Used especially to attract attention and to establish a
mood. Can be the featured materials and/or components of the design,
such as background or props.

"In" colors are a passing fad but are good ones to use at their time
of popularity.

"Warm" colors evoke a feeling of energy.

"Cool" colors establish a relaxed mood.

"Primary" (pure) colors can be combined to make "Secondary" (mixed)
colors.

"Value" is how light or dark a color is, and is described as:

"Tint," the process of making colors lighter, and
"Shade," the process of making colors darker.

"Intensity" is how bright or dull a color is.

"Color combinations" are chosen to be pleasing:

"Complementary" (opposite, contrast) colors are striking.
"Adjacent" (side-by-side, analogous) colors harmonize.
"Color Wheel" is the formal, established reference for contrast and analogous colors.

Stereotype feelings are significant regarding colors, e. g. : yellow is considered bright, sunny, cheerful; red is considered sensuous, exciting, dramatic.

2) <u>Line</u>: Placement of items to manipulate the direction in which the viewer's eyes will move while looking at the display. Line suggests an open element that is curved, diagonal, horizontal, or vertical. The line can be single, double, or multiple. (See Illus. 129.)

3) <u>Shape</u>: Formed by closing lines. Basic shapes can be two- or three-dimensional and include squares, rectangles, triangles, circles, ovals, and cubes. (See Illus. 130.)

4) <u>Size</u>: Small, medium, large dimensions. Location and combination of items to provide good visual balance or comparison. (See Illus. 131.)

5) <u>Texture</u>: The "feel" of a surface when it is viewed. Fabrics or objects, depending upon what they are made of, give the "impression" of being smooth, satiny, shiny, cool, rough (or nubby), dull, unpleasant.

6) <u>Weight</u>: The visual impression of "light" or "heavy" is influenced by size (bulk), color, shape, and texture. Larger, darker, nubbier (rougher) objects "seem" heavier than do smaller, brightly colored, smooth objects.

ELEMENTS

Physical Appearance (features) of What
Is Being Displayed

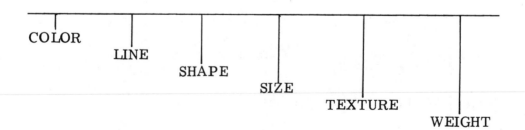

COLOR   LINE   SHAPE   SIZE   TEXTURE   WEIGHT

PRINCIPLES OF DISPLAY DESIGN: How the elements of design are used, singly or together, to attract viewers and to hold their attention.

1) Balance: Visual (optical) weight, which is influenced by the item's color, shape, and size.

   "Formal balance" is achieved by having both halves of the display be mirror images of each other (See Illus. 132.)

   "Informal Balance" is achieved by having each half of the display different from the other (See Illus. 133.)

2) Contrast: Using different combinations in color, shape, size, texture, and weight to draw attention to the display as a whole. (See Illus. 134.)

3) Emphasis: Handling the elements so as to focus the viewer's attention on key items in the display. (See Illus. 135.)

4) Harmony: The blending of the different elements to make the whole display pleasing and to make the message meaningful. (See the sketch in Illus. 136.)

5) Proportion: Using objects that fit together well in the available space. A feeling of being crowded is a poor use of proportion. (See Illus. 137.)

PRINCIPLES

Thoughtful Placement of Elements

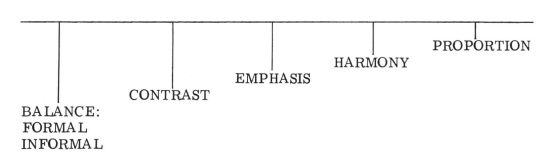

PROPORTION

HARMONY

EMPHASIS

CONTRAST

BALANCE:
FORMAL
INFORMAL

BASIC DISPLAY ARRANGEMENTS: Organization of the different parts of

displays within standard layouts.   Good use of display concepts is inher-
ent in each arrangement.

1) Fan: The eye is drawn to the single item at the bottom (base) and
   moves upward, or the eye is drawn to the single item in the front
   and moves back.   (See Illus. 138.)

2) Pyramid: The reverse of fan; the eye is drawn to the mass of items
   at the bottom (base) and moves upward, or to the mass of items in
   the front and moves to the back.   (See Illus. 139.)

3) Radiation: The eye is drawn to a single item in the center and moves
   to take in several items placed in a circle around it, as on a wheel
   or as rays or beams from the "sun."   (See Illus. 140.)

4) Repetition: The eye is attracted by the sheer mass of items placed
   in row after row or stack after stack in straight lines.   (See Illus.
   141.)

   Landscape is a variation of the repetitive arrangement in that specific
   patterns are repeated along a straight line.   (See Illus. 142.)

5) Step: The eye moves from the lowest to the highest step and can be
   featured sideways or from front to back in the display area.   (See
   Illus. 143.)

6) Zigzag: The eye is attracted to a controlled variety of placement.
   (See Illus. 144.)

DISPLAY CONSIDERATIONS: Decisions to make in the process of designing
   the display.

1) Access: Can everyone who is to see the display get to it and away
   from it easily?

2) Appeal: Is what you are putting on display something people want to
   look at?

   "Sales appeal" considerations dictate the location of the display.   A
   display on retirement activities will not do well in the YA section.

"Eye appeal" means displaying something that will attract attention simply because of what it is. Thus, props, coupled with books, are usually stronger lures than are books on their own.

"Time appeal" involves placing those items that are of current interest.

3) Depth: Can the display be made more interesting by changing the placement of items so that they are not on a flat surface or in a straight line in relation to each other? In Illus. 145, depth is achieved with a design on a flat surface. Illus. 146 suggests temporary or permanent "box 'n frame" display areas.

4) Focus: Is the position of the display such that people who view it from any number of perspectives continue to get the desired perceptions? (See "Shape" on next page.)

5) Framing: Is the area around the display correct for the design and contents of the display? (See "Location" below.)

6) Height: Is the vertical distance between the top and bottom correct for the design and for the items being put on display?

7) Location: Are the items being placed on display best put in a closed fixture or best left in an open area? For window displays, "open" means that individuals passing by the window can see the display and past it into the interior of the library; "closed" means that there is a partition that backs the display so that people see only the display and cannot see into the library. "Semi-closed" means that there is some screening, as with streamers, plants, open slats, or a sheer curtain. Other locations include tabletops and shelftops, racks, bins, carts, islands, platforms, walls, posts, ceiling, screens, easels, dividers, cases.

8) Motion: Would some sort of movement make the display more appealing? Motion can be created by motors that cause display components to fly, flow, or revolve, or by being hung in such a way that they are affected by the natural flow of air (as in mobiles).

9) Safety: Is the display designed so as to prevent injuries to viewers and damage to the items that are on display? Key points to check are electrical components, fire hazards, traffic flow, sharp edges and corners, falling or moving components that aren't supposed to fall off or move away, blocking of exits, glass that is not easily identifiable as glass, or poisonous items that young children may pop into their mouths.

10) <u>Shape</u>: Is the design in keeping with the best way to view the items being placed on display? The shape can be that the design is open from all sides, front open only, front and one side open, or front and two sides open. Illus. 147 suggests an unusual shape for a display area for flat objects, such as photographs, paintings, posters, or weaving.

11) <u>Timing</u>: Is the display going up at a time that will help build good public opinion and that will show the key materials off to their best advantage?

<u>DISPLAY COMPONENTS</u>: The parts that make up and unify a display design.

1) <u>Backgrounds</u>: Used to enhance the theme of the display for two-, and three-dimensional designs.

"Surfaces" include walls, screens, easels, and posts.

"Materials" include wallboard, fabrics, corrugated board, simulated wood grains, and fiberboard.

Illus. 148 shows a linking component of sturdy boards that can be re-arranged and reused as needed.

2) <u>Floor coverings</u>: Blend with the background and add to the theme.

"Surfaces" include not only floors of a room but also the bottom sur-face of cases, tabletops and shelf tops, platforms, and carts.

"Materials" include carpeting, cork chips, sand, rocks, grass or straw mats, woven materials, burlap, and felt.

3) <u>Lighting</u>: Used to make the entire display visible and to highlight spe-cific aspects of the design. Techniques include:

"Pinpointing"--a narrow beam of light that picks out a small item.
"Spotlighting"--a wide beam of light that picks out a large item.
"Floodlighting"--a combination of lights that covers an entire area.

4) <u>Merchandise</u>: In this case, items from the library collection or items that are being put on display within the library setting. This is the focal point of the display design and the reason for mounting the dis-play.

5) Props: Items in the display other than those that are the focus of attention.

"Functional props" are fixtures that hold or support the display merchandise.

"Standard functional props" in a library include plastic cases to hold such small items as magazines and pamphlets, book supports, open-book holders, expandable book caddies, wire book easels, metal book-rests, revolving book carousels, literature racks, portable easels, corkboards (open and with glass doors), conference cabinets (mounted and mobile), corkrail display strips, rollaway display shelves, bins, booktrucks, display cases, tables, racks and stands that are available from library suppliers. Other standard props are steps and risers. Bean bags of varying sizes are excellent display aids.

"Decorative props" are items that help carry out the theme of the display without serving as a support for key materials on display.

Illus. 149 indicates the use of props with appropriate materials. The display can be self-explanatory or you can add a sign that reads: "LET BOOKS GO TO YOUR HEAD. "

6) Sides and ceilings: Of special interest in closed cases and in window displays so that the entire area is a cohesive unit for the theme of the display.

7) Signs: Used to relay information that isn't communicated in the other display components. Some displays are self-sufficient. Others, however, need to make a statement in a headline.

"Show cards" carry the headline plus other information.

The lettering of the sign or show card and the manner in which it is mounted must adhere to the overall design of the display. Standard lettering materials include changeable letter boards, vinyl letters, gummed letter kits with guideline mounting boards, plastic display letters for corkboard and flat displays, pressure-sensitive letters, lettering kits, and sign-making machines.

Custom, or free-hand, lettering is an art that can be acquired through practice.

Signs can be laminated for durability and reuse.

Signs can be placed on easels, hung on lines, mounted on corkboards, positioned in poster-holders, held or supported by a prop or by the main materials on display, hung as a mobile, or placed in folded forms. Signs can also be hung as banners. (See Illus. 150, 151, and 152.)

Handy Resources for Display Components:

Flea markets   Houseware stores

Group or garage sales   General catalogs

Art-supply stores   Fabric stores

Hardware stores   Furniture stores

Library supply catalogs and agencies

Illus. 129.   LINE

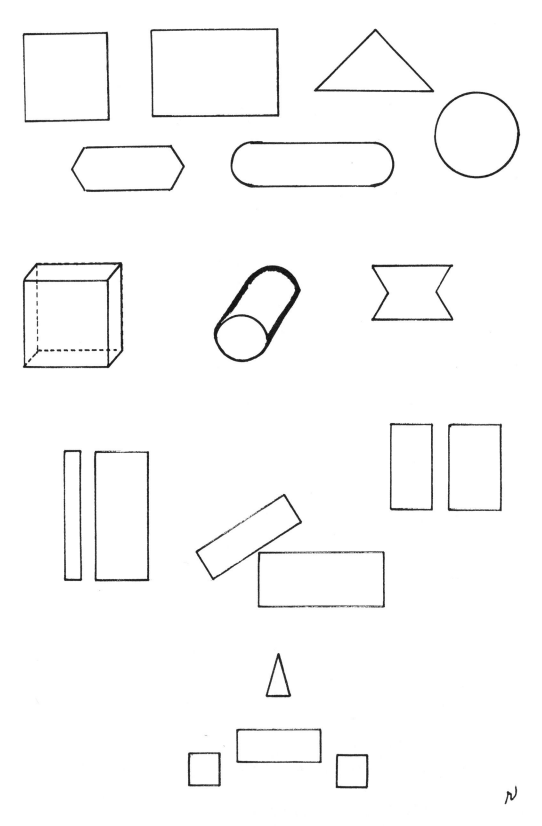

Illus. 130.   SHAPE

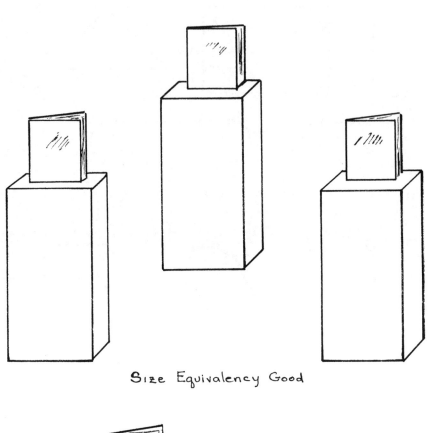

Size Equivalency Good

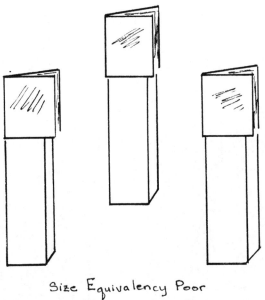

Size Equivalency Poor

Illus. 131.   SIZE: COMPARISON OF GOOD AND POOR USE

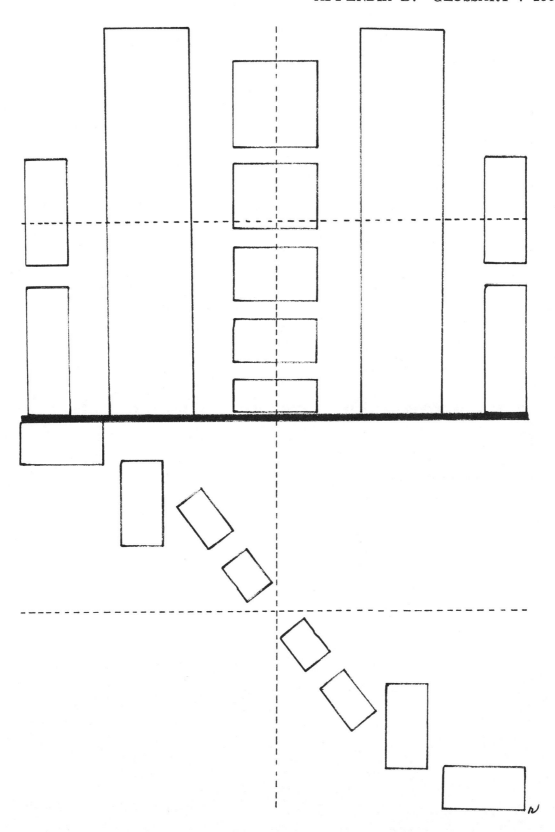

Illus. 132. FORMAL BALANCE

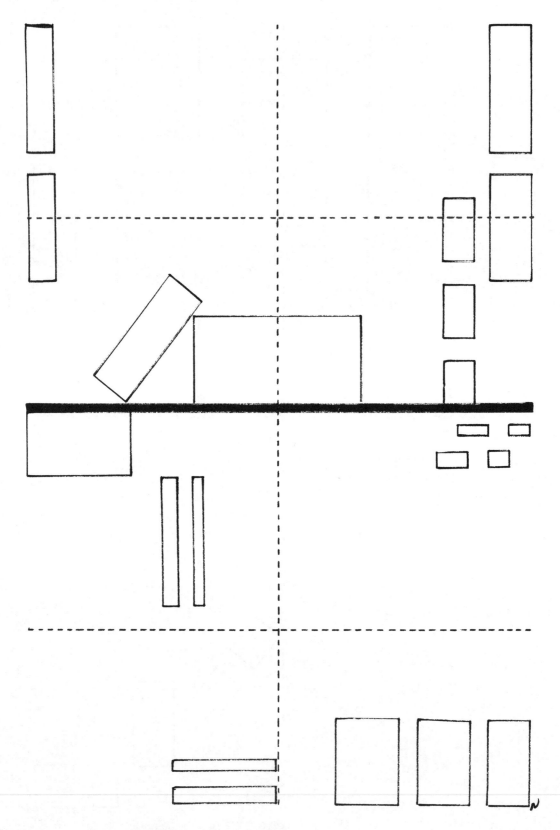

Illus. 133. INFORMAL BALANCE

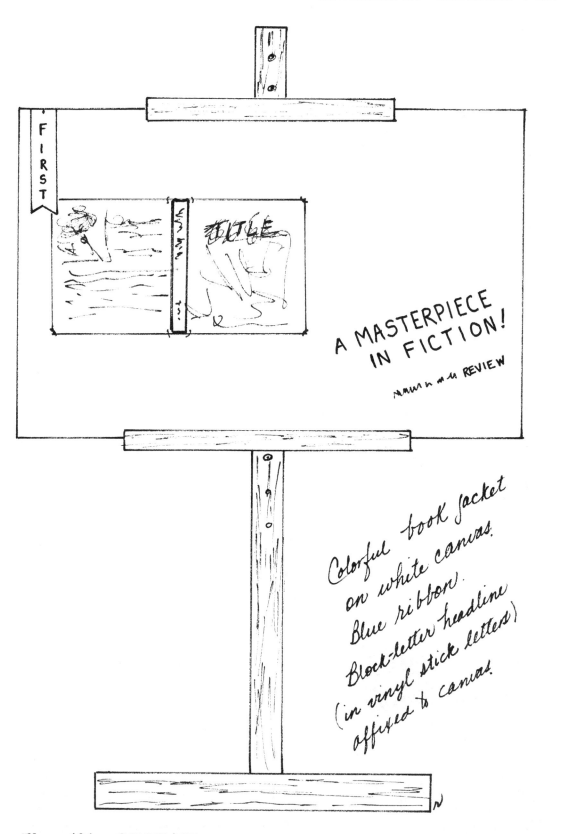

Illus. 134. CONTRAST

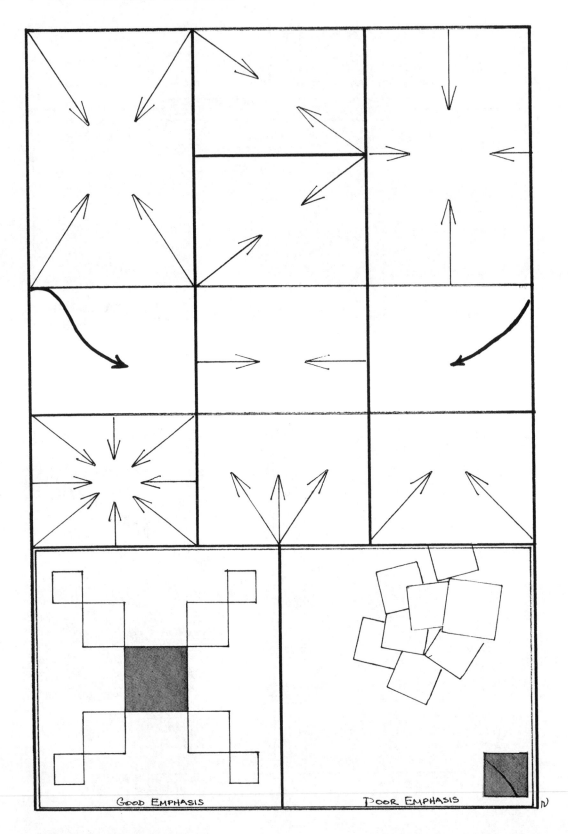

Illus. 135. EMPHASIS

DISPLAY ELEMENTS:
1) BOOK JACKETS OF TITLES RECORDED AS TALKING BOOKS PLACED AROUND
2) A TALKING-BOOK DISC, MOUNTED ON BRIGHT YELLOW FABRIC CIRCLE.
   DISC IS PULLED UP FOR A 3-D EFFECT.
3) BACKGROUND OF LIGHT BLUE FABRIC.
4) "HOT" LOOKING LETTERS PINNED AROUND YELLOW CIRCLE.

BOOKS ON DISC

BRIGHTEN EACH DAY

INQUIRE AT THE CIRCULATION DESK

Illus. 136. HARMONY

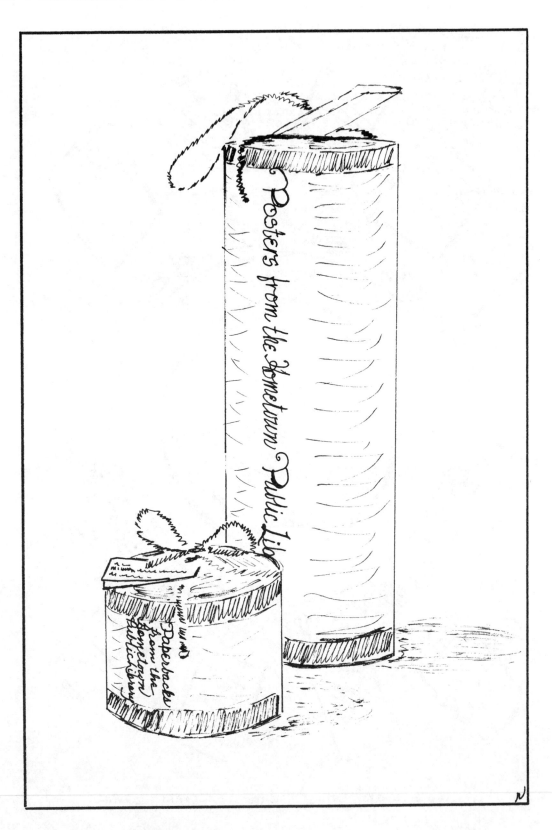

Illus. 137.   PROPORTION

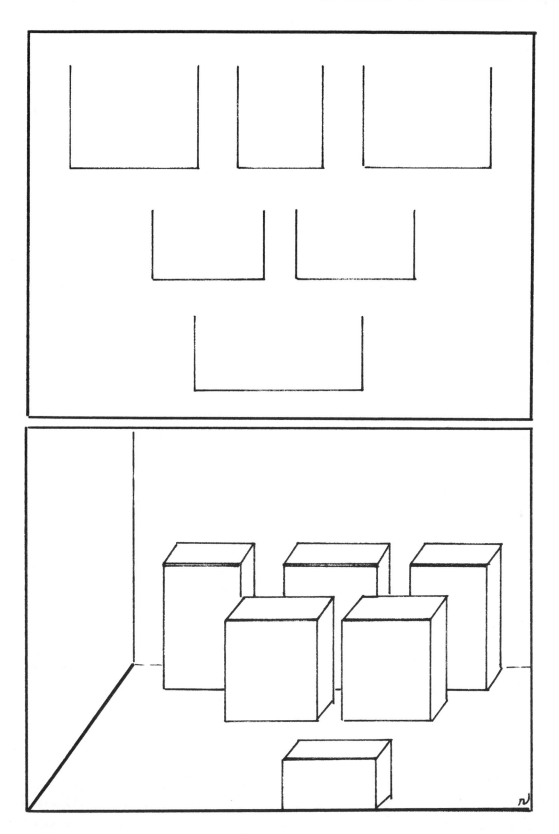

Illus. 138.   FAN ARRANGEMENTS

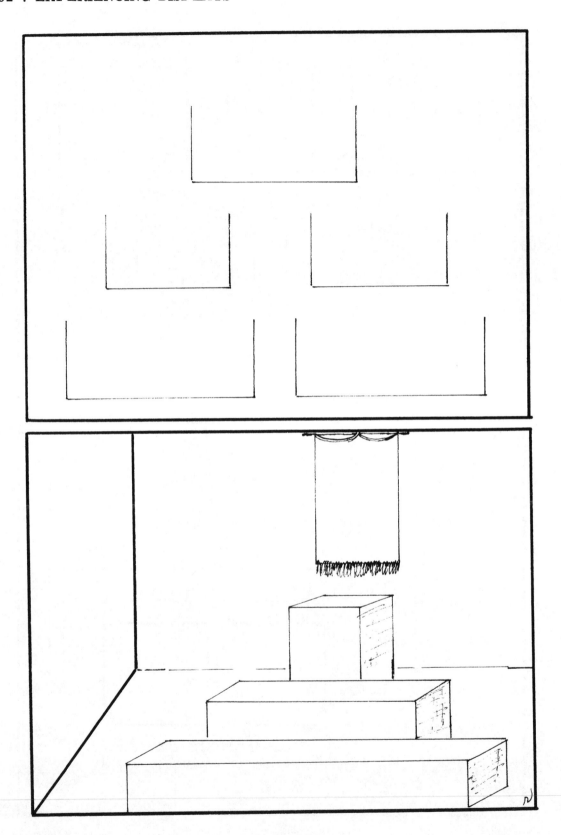

Illus. 139. PYRAMID ARRANGEMENTS

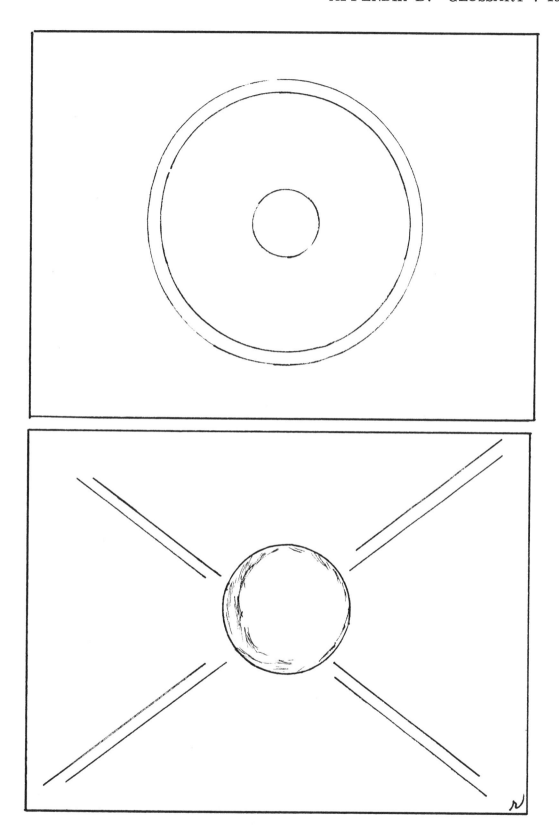

Illus. 140. RADIATION ARRANGEMENTS

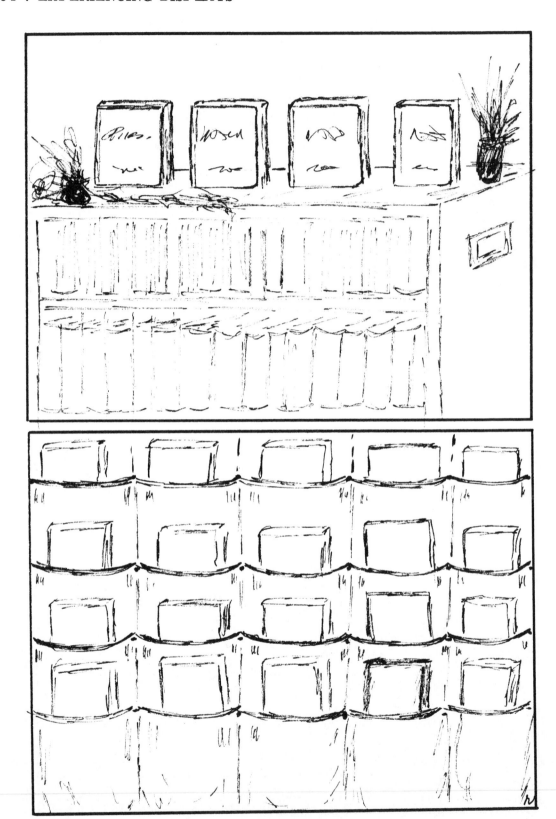

Illus. 141. REPETITION ARRANGEMENTS

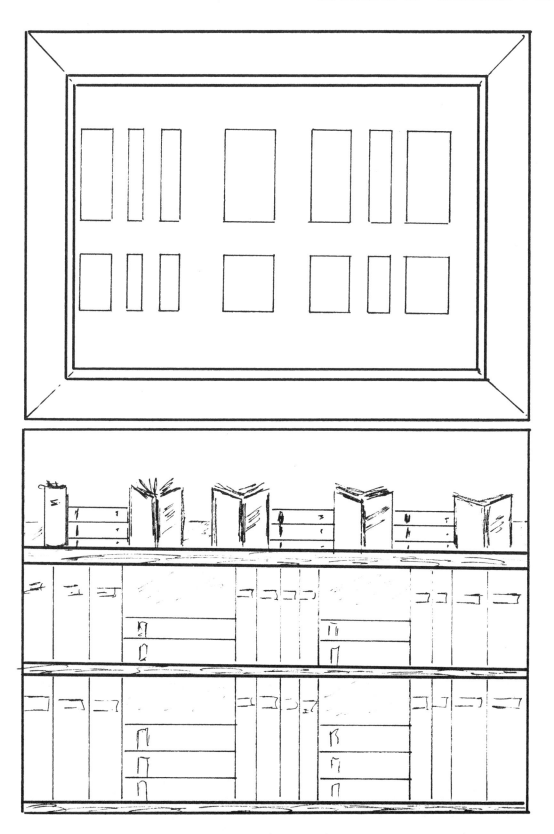

Illus. 142. LANDSCAPE ARRANGEMENTS

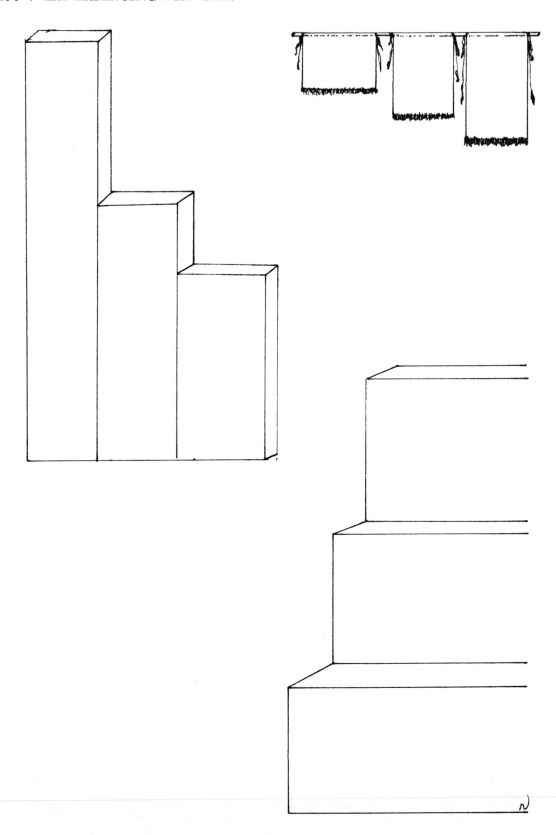

Illus. 143. STEP ARRANGEMENTS

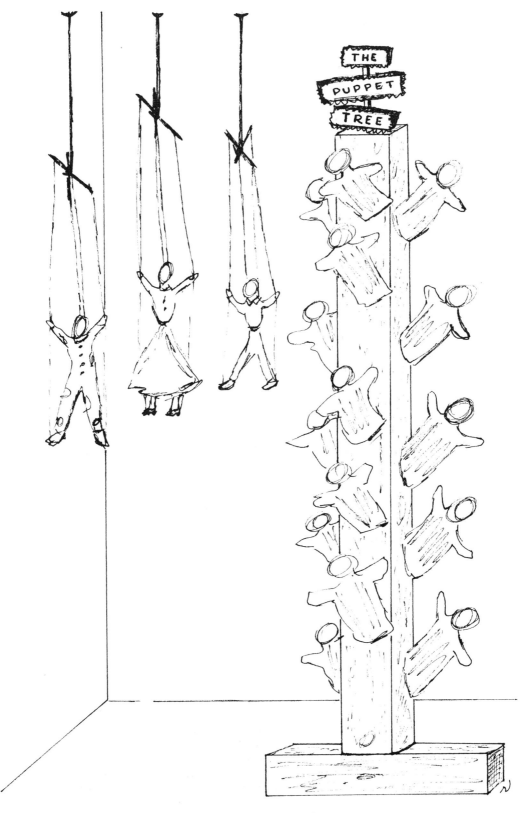

Illus. 144. ZIGZAG ARRANGEMENT: "THE PUPPET TREE"

Illus. 145.   DEPTH THROUGH DESIGN ON A FLAT SURFACE

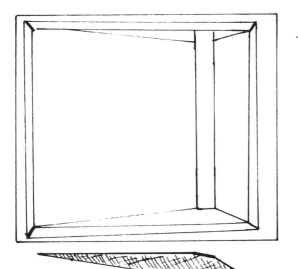

BUILD A FRAME
AROUND A
TRIANGULAR
SECTION TO
CREATE A
SHADOW-BOX
EFFECT THAT IS
DRAMATIC &
THAT SETS OFF
A DISPLAY
DIFFERENTLY
WITH DEPTH IN
A SMALL AREA.

TOP VIEW,
WITHOUT FRAME

BUILD A FRAME AROUND 2 BOXES
FOR AN IN-DEPTH DISPLAY AREA

Illus. 146.   DEPTH THROUGH FRAMED BOXES

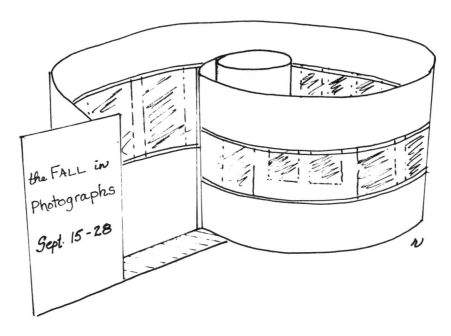

Illus. 147. UNUSUAL DISPLAY SURFACE

Illus. 148.　LINKING BOARDS

Illus. 149.   HATS HOLDING BOOKS

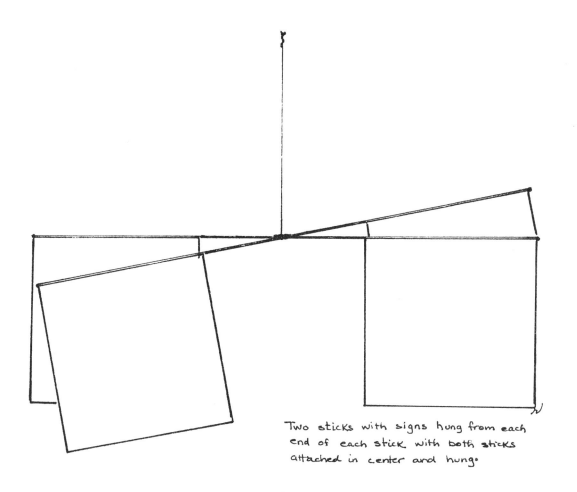

Two sticks with signs hung from each end of each stick with both sticks attached in center and hung.

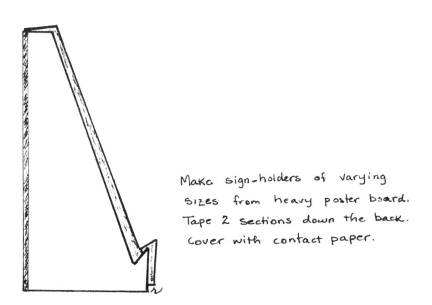

Make sign-holders of varying sizes from heavy poster board. Tape 2 sections down the back. Cover with contact paper.

Illus. 150.   IDEAS FOR SIGN HOLDERS

Illus. 151. EXAMPLES OF SIGNS

Illus. 152.   THERE'S MORE THAN ONE WAY TO SAY "READ"

Appendix C
PHOTOS OF LIBRARY DISPLAYS

The photographs in this Appendix speak for themselves. The narrative serves to identify their location.

Illus. 153-160 are of scenes in the Normal (Illinois) Public Library taken during the summer of 1981. The upper-left photo in Illus. 161 also is from the Normal Public Library. The upper-right photograph is of a window case at the University High School Media Center/Library in Normal, taken during the spring of 1981. The bottom photo is of a standing case display in the main children's reading room in the San Francisco Public Library (summer 1981).

Illus. 162 has three people-centered photos. "Stop for the Reading Hit Parade" features photos of participants in the summer-reading programs at the Normal Public Library. "Spring--Health, Sports, and Fitness" utilizes pictures of national personalities. It is a University High School Media Center/Library display. This brass quintet, in the bottom photo, is part of a cooperative effort between the Bloomington-Normal Symphony and the Normal Public Library during the summer of 1981.

Illus. 163 is of scenes in the main children's room of the San Francisco Public Library. The bottom photo attests to the durability of the "spark of childhood" that the fortunate among us carry into adulthood.

Illus. 153. SIGNS THAT IDENTIFY AND THAT DRUM UP BUSINESS

Illus. 154.   INFORMAL "INFORMATION CENTERS" AT ALL
ENTRANCES AND EXITS

Illus. 155.   SUMMERTIME, AN' THE READIN' IS SPOOKY

Illus. 156. MINI-DISPLAYS ON SHELF TOPS

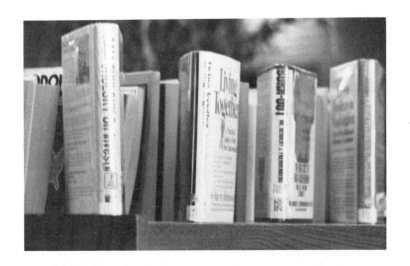

Illus. 157.   IF IT'S OUT, IT'LL ATTRACT ATTENTION

Illus. 158. THERE'S A PLACE, TOO, FOR AESTHETICS

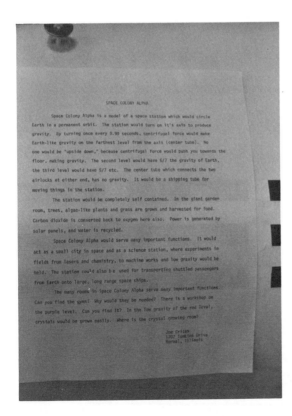

Illus. 159.   SPACE INTEREST: PATRON DISPLAY

Illus. 160. SUPERMAN IN DIORAMA: PATRON
DISPLAY

Illus. 161. CASE STUDIES

Illus. 162.   BRASS QUINTET: DISPLAY OF COOPERATION

Illus. 163. THE SPARK OF CHILDHOOD

INDEX